WOMEN IN SOCIETY
A Feminist List edited by
Jo Campling

The 1970s and 1980s have seen an explosion of publishing by, about and for women. This new list is designed to make a particular contribution to this process by commissioning and publishing books which consolidate and advance feminist research and debate in key areas in a form suitable for students, academics and researchers but also accessible to a broader general readership.

As far as possible books will adopt an international perspective incorporating comparative material from a range of countries where this is illuminating. Above all they will be interdisciplinary, aiming to put women's studies and feminist discussion firmly on the agenda in subject-areas as disparate as law, physical education, art and social policy.

A list of published and forthcoming titles follows overleaf

Women's Leisure, What Leisure?

Eileen Green, Sandra Hebron and Diana Woodward

MACMILLAN

First published 1990

Published by
MACMILLAN EDUCATION LTD
Houndmills, Basingstoke, Hampshire RG21 2XS
and London
Companies and representatives
throughout the world

Printed in Hong Kong

Edited and Typeset by Povey/Edmondson
Okehampton and Rochdale, England

British Library Cataloguing in Publication Data
Green, Eileen *1947–*
Women's leisure, what leisure? —(Women in society).
1. Great Britain. Women. Leisure activities
I. Title   II. Woodward, Diana   III. Hebron, Sandra   IV.
Series
306.48088042
ISBN 0–333–43518–4 (hardcover)
ISBN 0–333–43519–2 (paperback)

Series Standing Order

If you would like to receive future titles in this series as they
are published, you can make use of our standing order
facility. To place a standing order please contact your
bookseller or, in case of difficulty, write to us at the address
below with your name and address and the name of the
series. Please state with which title you wish to begin your
standing order. (If you live outside the UK we may not have
the rights for your area, in which case we will forward your
order to the publisher concerned.)

Standing Order Service, Macmillan Distribution Ltd,
Houndmills, Basingstoke, Hampshire, RG21 2XS, England

Contents

Acknowledgements

We would like to thank all those who helped in the preparation of this book. It would not have been written without the funding for the research project on which it is based being provided by the Sports Council/Economic and Social Research Council Joint Panel. Members of the Steering Group attached to the project provided us with invaluable advice and support along the way. Special thanks go to Vivienne Mallinder, who worked as secretary to the project; the work involved hours of transcription of tapes, typing the manuscripts, and giving advice and feedback on the research itself. Her patience and sense of humour meant a lot to us. Many colleagues and friends shared their own work with us, offering advice and support when things went wrong – particularly Jackie Burgoyne, whose premature death in January 1988 saddened us all. The weekend workshop in 1985 at the Centre for Leisure Research, Dunfermline College of Physical Education, and several feminist gatherings at the Brighton International Leisure Studies Conferences renewed our confidence in the theoretical approach. Special thanks go to Ian Atkinson, Celia Brackenridge, Mike Maher and Mark Parkin for support and help in keeping it all in perspective, and to Sam, Alexander, Nicholas and Zoë for putting up with us thinking about leisure rather than doing it. Finally we are indebted to many women in Sheffield who so generously shared their ideas and personal experiences with us in the research on which parts of this book are based.

EILEEN GREEN
SANDRA HEBRON
DIANA WOODWARD

Introduction

The impetus for this book was our irritation and confusion about the over-defined concept of leisure. It seemed at its least relevant when applied to the lives of the majority of women, as they juggled children, domestic lives and jobs, and attempted to squeeze in 'time for themselves'. We ourselves were no exception, we wryly observed, as we struggled to write about leisure amid the competing demands of employment, children and long-suffering partners! During the writing the leisure services boom has intensified, with local authorities joining the race to provide upmarket leisure 'palaces' modelled on the revolutionary Whitley Bay experiment of the 1970s – a British leisure pool equipped with wave machine, water slides and assorted tropical 'forests'. Prophets of this approach to meeting our leisure 'needs' enjoyed a high profile at the 1988 International Leisure Studies Conference at Brighton, where the audience were subjected to a mesmerising visual display of leisure 'worlds' encapsulated in heated glass domes. Alert members of the audience considered the reactions of elderly users of community leisure facilities: would they approve of such hi-tech replacements to their neighbourhood pools, assuming they could afford the entrance fee? The feminists among us wondered cynically where 'Mum' fitted into this picture of glamour and self-actualisation. Was she changing nappies in the non-existent creche, or chatting to the other women as they observed their offspring braving the delights of the water slides?

The theoretical approach developed throughout the book is informed by our commitment to feminism, together with a socialist perspective through which we attempt to analyse the social structures within which women's leisure experiences are set. It is our contention that feminist approaches to leisure have reached a critical stage, characterised by the beginnings of debate among feminists on differences of theory and related politics. The critique of traditional approaches within leisure studies is now paralleled by a collective concern to shape feminist perspectives which both 'allow women a voice' and provide a framework with which to analyse major changes (see Wimbush and Talbot (1988) for a more detailed discussion of different feminist perspectives on women's leisure). In Chapter 1 we map out such theoretical developments.

Whilst leisure theorists and journalists suggest that leisure as a way of defining oneself has become somewhat 'déclassé' now that unemployment means there is so much of it around, the leisure industry feverishly competes to come up with the ultimate leisure experience. This will no doubt be enjoyed by the fabled 'dinkies' (dual income, no kids) and 'yuppies' (young, upwardly mobile professional people), who are young, white, middle class and primarily male. The regeneration of British industry is highly dependent upon the expansion of the service industries, with the development of new personal services ranging from dinner parties to house sitting – services which seem to combine the gentility of Victorian England with the efficiency of contemporary Manhattan. Labour market statistics tell us that the bulk of workers employed in these new industries are, and increasingly will be, women, whose share of the job market is predicted to rise to 50 per cent by the 1990s, with most of the increase in the area of part-time employment. If more women are taking on paid work in addition to domestic responsibilities and childcare, their opportunities to partake of the new leisure experience will be even more constrained than they are at present. A body of evidence exists to confirm that women generally have less time, resources and opportunities for leisure than men (Deem, 1986a; Wimbush, 1986; Wearing and Wearing, 1988) and a narrower range of options on where and with whom to spend it (Green, Hebron and Woodward, 1987b).

In order to explore the issue of leisure for women we need to examine it in context, noting the current increases in part-time employment rates which appear to offer flexibility and therefore choices, until the anti-social hours and low rates of pay are considered (Beechey and Perkins, 1987). Also noteworthy is the phenomenon of 'teleworking' – working from home with the tools of information technology, which involves mainly women as paid workers, or unpaid workers servicing the work of male partners. Teleworking is portrayed by employers as 'liberating' more time to spend with the family, which ignores the well-known fact that women are more likely than men to be involved in homeworking anyway, whether paid (Allen and Wolkowitz, 1987) or unpaid. Shifting employment back into the domestic sphere will undoubtedly reduce employers' overheads, but is also likely to reduce further women's free time – time that is potentially available for leisure.

This book aims critically to address the issue of women's leisure, drawing upon research data collected during a three-year project on gender and leisure funded jointly by the English Sports Council and the Economic and Social Research Council.

Our analysis developed out of a study of women's leisure in Sheffield, carried out between 1984 and 1987. Our interest has been not so much in the amount and type of leisure that women engage in, but in the cultural significance of leisure, an issue which clearly has a gender dimension. We are also concerned with leisure as a site of potential conflict, which highlights the contradictory nature of the 'freedom' and 'pleasure' labels traditionally attached to it. Leisure cannot be compartmentalised and explored in isolation from other parts of life, as the character of its vital ingredients – time, resources and commitment – are indicative of the broader social structures within which they emerge; for women that generally involves a web of inequalities. A woman's right to freedom in leisure is circumscribed by her employment status and income level, her family situation and, most important, her lack of status as a woman in a patriarchal society.

The structure of the book encompasses these broad themes; they appear in each chapter and are explored from a variety of perspectives. Chapter 2 builds upon the theoretical premises outlined in the first chapter, and attempts to move towards an understanding of leisure from a socialist feminist perspective. To this end we draw significantly upon cultural studies in order to explore the connections between cultural forms, ideology and class relations, assessing their impact upon patriarchy. A crucial historical dimension is provided in Chapter 3, which traces the social history of women's leisure. Uncovering this history is no easy task, owing to the grave lack of published material. Oral histories, diaries and biographies are among the richest sources, as Stanley notes in her recent discussion of historical accounts of women's leisure (in Wimbush and Talbot, 1988). Such informal accounts combine rich personal experiences with reflections on the changing social fabric within which they took place. Chapter 4 reviews existing data on women's leisure patterns, drawing extensively on our own research material and placing it within a broad, comparative context through the use of both quantitative and qualitative evidence. The most fascinating part of this evidence appears in the form of personal accounts, for example of the operation of gendered social control processes in relation to leisure. This process is explored in depth in Chapter 5, which also examines the centrality of sexuality in negotiations between women and their male partners about women's access to independent leisure outside the home. Sexuality is a crucial component of ideological representations of women, both in pursuing their own leisure interests and in servicing the leisure of others. We argue that it is this component that accounts for the often highly charged nature of gender relations, in private negotiations about how and with whom women spend their leisure time, and in public leisure venues where women are often indiscriminately viewed as part of the entertainment. Chapter 7 attempts to draw together some of the positive attempts to improve and extend women's leisure opportunities. The discussion ranges from an analysis of good practice in leisure provision by public and private agencies, to informal strategies which rely heavily on time-honoured female networks of women friends, relatives and neighbours.

Substantial sections of the book involve a detailed examination of the structural constraints that operate to limit both the form and frequency of women's leisure opportunities. However, we are also concerned to emphasise the importance of leisure as a rich source of pleasure and continuity in the lives of many of the women we interviewed. A night out for a 'laugh with the girls' is a jealously guarded pursuit which counteracts social isolation and reinforces the female solidarity that has endured across time and cultures of difference.

In conducting the study of Sheffield women's leisure experiences we sought to operate as a team, with non-hierarchical working practices. This book is likewise the product of a genuine collaborative effort, although the subsequent dispersal of team members to other jobs and research projects has made this ideal increasingly difficult to realise. The ideas expressed here are by and large shared by us all; as far as the writing is concerned, Eileen Green was primarily responsible for the Introduction and Chapters 1 and 6, Sandra Hebron for Chapters 2 and 3 and the Conclusion, and Diana Woodward for Chapters 4, 5 and 7.

1

Conceptualising leisure

Introduction

Leisure has a chameleon-like quality, changing its skin in relation to surroundings, context and the seriousness of its competitors. A young mother collecting her thoughts over a cup of tea while her children are asleep can be just as much 'at leisure' as the newly appointed executive enjoyed a celebratory lunch with her female colleagues at a city-centre wine bar. For most individuals it is the quality of the experience that is important, rather than the venue or the activity, and the chance it affords for 'a break', a 'change' or 'time to be yourself'. This chapter takes a critical look at the treatment of gender issues within leisure studies and attempts to locate a feminist analysis of women's leisure within the general context of recent theoretical developments in the field.

Our interest in the sociology of leisure stems from a general dissatisfaction with the treatment of women in the sociological perspectives emerging in Britain in the late 1960s, a dissatisfaction summed up by Ann Oakley in an early and now classic feminist critique of British sociology (Oakley, 1974). This involved a critique of the male-dominated approach which characterised the sociology of work and industry (Green and Woodward, 1977) and a gradual realisation that the artificial separation of areas of life entitled 'work' and 'leisure' into different subsections of the discipline both marginalised the experiences of women and obscured the significant 'overlaps' that happen in real life. In Britain, as in the USA, this early unease with prevailing mainstream perspectives stimulated the development of a general feminist critique of sociology, through the compilation of empirical evidence which contradicted the new orthodoxies and led to the articulation of new feminist theories.

In 1983 two of us were encouraged to apply for the contract to undertake a study of gender and leisure being commissioned by the English Sports Council/Economic and Social Research Council Joint Panel on Leisure and Recreation Research. The results of this study, based on a survey and interviews with 700 Sheffield women, have been published in report form (Green, Hebron and Woodward, 1987b) and comprise a body of evidence drawn upon throughout the book. (The project is discussed in more detail later in this chapter.) The report argues, first, for a theoretical framework which emphasises the importance of gender divisions and, second, for employing a range of research methods to construct an empirical account of women's leisure. Gender divisions are crucial in the maintenance and reproduction of the unequal, patriarchal social relations characteristic of modern capitalism, and women's leisure cannot be adequately understood outside the social and political context within which it is located. Thus we need to engage in a theoretical analysis of both the material constraints and the ideological processes that influence the social organisation of leisure generally, and the specific forms which women's leisure takes. This perspective, developed during the Sheffield study, has informed the approach taken in this book.

'It doesn't apply to women': definitions of leisure

The problems encountered in attempting to define leisure have been well documented, both by theorists working within traditional leisure studies and sociology of leisure perspectives (Parker, 1971, 1976; Roberts, 1970) and more recently by feminists and others engaged in the study of women's leisure (Stanley, 1980; Gregory, 1982; Stockdale, 1985; Wimbush, 1986). We cannot escape the insoluble problem of defining leisure, because therein lies the justification for studying it. Undertaking a major research project on the study of women's leisure thus entailed an early confrontation with the 'what is leisure?' question. This became translated into a familiar refrain that we were to hear so often in response to our attempts to elicit information: 'women's leisure, what leisure?' This phrase, we learned, denoted a double-edged confusion: first with the concept itself, and second when it was applied to women.

The term 'leisure' conjures up a hazy vision of endless time to pursue the pleasure(s) of one's choosing in the form and quantity required to satisfy personal appetites – necessarily an individualised menu and one which defies generalised definition. Having said that, Britain in the early 1980s was portrayed by policy-makers and providers as becoming a 'leisure society' which promised greater freedom from paid work. Leisure was portrayed by some as having a new set of functions and acting as ' *a mediator of social change* with the dual role of securing continuity in people's lives while acting as a source of innovation' (Sports Council/ESRC, 1985. 1, original emphasis). This vision appears to have dimmed somewhat as we approach the end of the decade, with little sign of paid work vacating centre-stage position as the major indicator of social class, income and identity. Leisure viewed in context involves placing it within a capitalist society characterised by shifting relations between employment, work and leisure, a major determinant of such relations being economic and ideological forces which are themselves historically constituted. High levels of unemployment may indeed mean that for an increasing proportion of the population, paid work either never has occupied or no longer occupies most of their time; but naively to portray the absence of paid work as freedom is to ignore the potential privations attached to unemployment in a society where status derives from income and wealth.

Common elements of attempts to define leisure include the ingredients of pleasure and free choices, together with clearly demarcated periods of time, and are usually contrasted with non-voluntary activities such as paid work and everyday commitments. Debates about the usefulness and pertinence of the concept of leisure are ongoing (Roberts, 1983; Rojek, 1985; Deem, 1986a) and demonstrate the changing points of interest and concern within the field of leisure studies. Theorists and researchers have only recently begun to recognise the significance of gender (and race), which has added to the problems of definition and remains little more than a token recognition in an area where patriarchal perspectives are paramount (Wimbush and Talbot, 1988).

Defining leisure in relation to paid work and the assumption that everyone has access to periods (however limited) of 'free time', present a range of problems when it comes to women's leisure. Adequate theorisations of women's leisure do not dichotomise paid work and leisure; rather they examine it in the context of women's lives as a whole. Gregory (1982) notes that it is important to establish the meaning of leisure in women's lives. Leisure has an important historical dimension, being culturally defined and constructed. Our initial preoccupation in the Sheffield study was to discover how women define and understand leisure, and how far it is a meaningful concept for them. What does 'leisure', a term traditionally applied to time free from paid work, mean in the context of women's lives? What potential contradictions exist between broad social definitions of leisure and women's experiences?

Putting women first

As feminists involved in research about women we were concerned to adopt an approach which places women in the foreground whilst recognising them as an oppressed group with certain interests in common. This perspective heavily influenced both the theoretical position adopted and the methodology used to obtain data on women's leisure, although we would agree with Rosemary Deem that:

> there is no *one* feminist approach. Although all feminists would agree that women are oppressed, they would certainly have disagreements about the determinants of that oppression and the mechanisms through which it operates as well as the strategies for change. (Deem, 1986, p. 11)

The inclusion or not of the concept of patriarchy is a central point of difference, particularly for those feminists attempting to use a socialist feminist framework. A well-established debate on this topic is summarised by Eisenstein (1979) and Barrett (1980) in a general discussion of Marxist/socialist feminist theory. Although we argue that patriarchy is fundamental to our analysis, defining it as the domination of women through systems of power and control which ultimately privilege men, we also stress the historical dimension, recognising the significance of changes in the form and cultural emphasis of leisure. Because the issue of women's own understandings of leisure was so central to the study, we attempted to explore it at each stage of the project in order to highlight ways in which the meaning of leisure may vary, depending in part upon women's cultural background and current situation.

During the early group discussions with local women it emerged that leisure is not a term that most women would use to describe or refer to parts of their lives. This confirms the findings of Dixey and Talbot (1982), Wimbush (1986) and Deem (1986a). Many of the women found it difficult to define leisure, seeing it as a vague and amorphous concept. Most could not provide a general definition, but found it meant more to them when related directly to specific activities. Those who did provide general definitions, however, shared what seemed at first sight to be a surprisingly high degree of consensus. Closer scrutiny showed their responses to embody widely held, common-sense assumptions about what constitutes leisure, and there was often a gap between the formal definition offered and the ways in which related activities were described. In the survey women were asked an open-ended question about their understanding of 'leisure time'. The most typical responses were statements such as: 'Time spent on anything that you enjoy' and 'Free time when you can do whatever you want.' The notions of enjoyment and pleasure, particularly the opportunity to 'please yourself', were central to most of the definitions given. Leisure for women is less linked to what are traditionally perceived as leisure activities than to a special state of mind or quality of experience. One explanation for this could be that much of women's experience of what is popularly seen as leisure actually involves them in varying degrees of work (Talbot, 1979). Servicing the leisure of others, both materially and emotionally, leaves little time for their own relaxation. One woman's description of her experience of Sundays, the traditional day free from work, sums it up:

I used to say that Sundays were boring, but since we've had kids, I think Sundays are the busiest days that there is. That's when everyone's at home you see, you don't have a minute.

I hate Sundays!

Leisure is clearly seen to involve at least some individual autonomy and choice. Linked with this is the widely held belief that leisure is characterised by freedom from obligation or constraint, though this is not to suggest that leisure is conceived of as a wholly residual category.

Relaxation

The concept of relaxation was frequently mentioned as being central to any definition of women's leisure. It was generally presented as fundamentally a recuperative activity, a way of physically or mentally recharging one's batteries. Indeed, one of the key elements in leisure was seen to be the opportunity it provides for some rest and recovery from the demands of everyday life. Women mentioned a huge variety of activities, ranging from gardening to 'doing nothing', which fulfil this function for them. But as Deem (1986a) comments in her discussion of 'at-home leisure', the overlaps between leisure and work in the home make it impossible to define leisure on an activity basis. In a similar way to the Sheffield study, Deem found that:

> activities such as knitting, sewing, gardening and cooking were extremely popular leisure activities and seen as enjoyable but only under certain conditions. So gardening is enjoyable when it involves creating a rock-garden or tending well-loved plants on a sunny day with a whole afternoon available, but not when it means taming an overgrown lawn on an overcast evening as well as cooking tea, washing three machine-loads of clothes, cleaning the kitchen and bathing children! (Deem, 1986a, p. 34)

The single defining characteristic of all activities mentioned by the Sheffield women was that they should constitute a 'change', something different from normal routines and the obligations of day-to-day living. In addition, for some women, most notably those with children, relaxation was inextricably linked with 'solitude', with the opportunity to have time and space for oneself, free from the interruptions or demands of others. Several of the women with young children commented on how leisure for them really only exists once the children are in bed (and asleep):

> I class leisure as the time when I've not got [my daughter] because she's my sort of work at the moment, and it's nice to know she's gone to bed and I can do what I want for a couple of hours.

In some cases wives actively encourage husbands to go out in the evenings, this being the only time when they can begin to relax.

Sociability

A further dimension which many women feel is important in defining leisure is sociability – the opportunity to mix with other people. Whilst relaxation was clearly perceived to be an important and necessary part of leisure, it seems that for many of the women 'real leisure' should offer the opportunity for having fun in company, usually outside the home environment. This is one area that can be a source of conflict. In the Sheffield survey, 11 per cent of the women with partners said they would like to go out more often with their partner, but that he was unwilling. Several of the women we interviewed reported that on returning home after a day's work, their husbands preferred to spend their evenings in the home:

> I used to want to go out because I do like socialising. My husband used to work outside and when he came home all he wanted was his armchair and the television.

This was frustrating for women who had already spent most of the day at home.

In some cases where joint leisure with partners offers little opportunity for lively social interaction, women are able to have 'girls' nights out', which offer the chance to 'have a laugh and a chat'. In the discussion groups women compared nights out with other women with nights out in mixed company. The general feeling was that being in all-women company offered opportunities for 'letting your hair down' and discussing personal experiences:

> we'll put the world to rights, we'll discuss our sexual problems if there are any, have a laugh, talk terrible about our husbands . . .

This kind of discussion between women has a clear role in how they come to understand and make sense of their experiences and problems:

> . . . and its nice to know that everybody's in the same position that you are. That's when you realise that you're no different.

It is worth noting that, for many women, being in company is the most important element in nights out, with the kind of leisure venues or specific activities being of a secondary nature:

> Oh, it doesn't matter where we go, we could sit in the middle of a tip, it doesn't matter. It's just being with them, that's what matters.

Just over half the women in the survey reported that they enjoy spending time talking to friends and neighbours, and will go out of their way to do this.

The high emphasis which women place on sociability means that for many of them paid work offers considerable scope for leisure-like experiences. These can range from chatting at meal or break times or while working, through celebrating birthdays and other special events, or weekly trips to the pub at lunchtime, to more organised parties or outings. Even where women do not spend any out-of-work time with workmates, sociability is felt to be an important aspect of paid work, and for some of the Sheffield women it is the main reason why they continue or return to employment despite the heavy dual workload this may involve:

> I do like being with people, and wouldn't like to be without a job, without that sort of contact.

For other women, employed in boring or monotonous jobs because of financial need, the opportunity to chat with workmates helps to make the work itself more tolerable.

Although paid employment can impinge upon leisure, none of the women we spoke to in the interview stage felt that it had particularly restrictive consequences for leisure. Some women felt that it had little effect, seeing their leisure as a separate sphere involving partners, relatives and friends from outside work. The remainder felt that paid employment had improved both their social life and the quality of their life in general by providing greater opportunities for social contact and for the development of interests outside the home and family:

> I've made a lot more friends since I've been going out to work, met a lot more people.

We will be returning to this issue of the relationship between women's paid employment and their leisure opportunities in Chapter 5.

The work-leisure dichotomy

Despite the excessive preoccupation of traditional leisure theorists with the arena of paid work, and their concomitant failure to see housework and childcare as real work, almost all the women we interviewed used work as an elastic term which could take in both paid employment and domestic work. However, women in full-time paid work were more likely to conceptualise leisure as discrete periods of non-work time than other women. In general they find it easier to 'compartmentalise' areas of their lives than women who work in the home.

In the Sheffield study this was particularly so for young single women who defined leisure in contrast to work. For them leisure usually meant

> forgetting about work, relaxing, doing what I want to do, seeing who I want to see. (single woman, aged 20)

However, work could sometimes be experienced as leisure by women with heavy domestic and childcare commitments, especially when it involved the chance for a rare outing:

> As I say, a visit to the market is an outing for me. (woman with youngest child, aged 7 months)

> My mum's got a pub and I work Saturday nights there and I enjoy that. I find it's like a night out, a complete change, meeting people. I'm me, I'm not someone's mum or somebody's wife and customers don't know that I go home and wash nappies, just a complete change. (woman with two children)

Over a quarter of the respondents defined leisure as 'time doing anything except work', with this proportion being highest among women with few domestic commitments.

In addition, many of the women spent a significant amount of their leisure time on activities which they recognised could be defined as work, such as gardening, sewing, and so on. The pleasure which women find in these activities was frequently attributed to the element of freedom involved in choosing them. Women do them from choice rather than from obligation. As one woman we interviewed put it:

> There's pleasure in both leisure and work, but somehow, always at the back of your mind . . . when you think of work you think of something that you're being paid to do.

The activities themselves were particularly enjoyed when they involved departure from daily routines and the opportunity to be creative, something which many women felt was missing in other areas of life.

Women in full-time paid employment were more likely to consider cooking and some other domestic tasks as being leisure-like, compared with women in part-time employment or non-employed women. In the survey the majority of household tasks tended to be seen as 'neither work nor leisure' but as containing elements of each. However, when we developed this in the interview stage it became clear that although women felt they had some autonomy in organising domestic work, the tasks themselves generally constitute work. For some women it is the difference between paid and unpaid work that is the source of pleasure. Furthermore, there are very clear differences in the leisure-like qualities of various functions within each task, for example between cooking a 'special' meal to entertain friends and the obligation to provide a nourishing but inexpensive family meal each evening. This highlights the inadequacy of seeking to define activities as either 'work' or 'leisure'. In women's lives such boundaries as do exist are likely to be complex, blurred and shifting. Developing a more adequate conceptualisation of leisure than those used by traditional leisure studies theorists involves a parallel critique of male-dominated theoretical approaches which render women's leisure invisible. It is to such approaches that we now turn.

Theoretical perspectives on leisure

This section is not an attempt to provide a comprehensive review of leisure theory, as this has already been done elsewhere (for example, Clarke and Critcher, 1985). Instead our purpose is to provide a brief review of the literature in sufficient detail to outline the context of recent feminist theoretical critiques and empirical research, in order to indicate the paradigms and assumptions that they seek to challenge.

Traditional leisure studies and the 'founding fathers'

Images of leisure as the antithesis of work have firm historical roots in an industrial society which, since the nineteenth century, has been characterised by the close regulation of working hours and little intrinsic satisfaction available from work itself for the majority of the population. The attendant frustrations of increased mechanisation, fragmentation and routinisation of work have been fully explored by industrial psychologists (McGregor, 1960; Herzberg, 1965), who were often employed by firms in the private sector intent upon achieving better personnel relations with their workers. More recently emphasis has shifted to analyses of 'user-involvement' strategies in the area of new technology (Mumford and Sademan, 1975; Weir, 1977; SPRU, 1982) with the most radical perspectives taking account of gender issues (Cockburn, 1983; Game and Pringle, 1984; Volst and Wagner, 1986; Liff, 1988).

It is no accident that leisure should emerge as an area for study within the context of social science perspectives on industry (Parker *et al.*, 1972). The most cursory analysis of leisure studies in their historical context readily reveals this as the background to leisure conceptualised as compensation for the privations endured at work. This view remains remarkably persistent, despite its irrelevance to huge sections of society today and its uneasy 'fit' with one contemporary vision which sees purposeful leisure operating as an antidote to mass unemployment.

Despite a growing recognition of leisure as a sub-discipline within sociology, studies in the area are still relatively marginalised and often ignored altogether in general textbooks, or are included as a subsection of chapters on paid work. The 'Founding Fathers' of the sociology of leisure in Britain emerged with the publication of their textbooks on leisure in the early 1970s, most notably Stanley Parker and Kenneth Roberts. Before that, students and researchers in the area were limited to American material of a functionalist nature (for example Gross, 1961) or philosophical writings on the relationship between human nature and the need to play (Huizinga, 1950).

Exceptions to this lay in the area of empirical sociology, a good example of which are the British community studies, which concentrated on traditional working-class communities (Young and Willmott, 1957; Dennis, Henriques and Slaughter, 1969). Such studies examined the nature of everyday life, emphasising the close social interaction within the community, and leisure was depicted as a vital part of community life. Some of these studies are re-examined in Chapter 5 to see what information they offer about women's leisure experiences. A similar focus upon leisure patterns is found in the work of theorists in the area known as 'cultural criticism' (Hoggart, 1958; Williams, 1962). Within this framework, the working-class community was analysed as one part of class-based culture, the formation of which was viewed as an ongoing dynamic social process. Leisure is a key area where class-related attitudes and social practices are shaped and transformed. However, both community studies and cultural criticism were, and still are in effect, marginal to mainstream sociology. The ethnographic contribution that could be made to leisure studies from these sources has remained largely embryonic.

Throughout the 1970s the preoccupations of the literature in the leisure field were issues of tangential relevance to women's situation. As argued above, leisure was defined in terms of its antithesis to paid work as time largely free from external constraints, which a person could freely choose to spend as he or she wished (Parker, 1971). This conceptual starting point led to a heavy concentration in both theoretical and empirical work on white male workers' class position, occupational cultures and associated leisure activities. Women, in so far as they featured at all, appeared as the partners of the men studied, and yet the findings were presented as axioms of general relevance and applicability (Parker, 1971; Dunning, 1971; Salaman, 1974). Parker, for example, writes: 'in considering the various categories we have had in mind men in full-time employment. Certain modifications to the scheme are necessary if it is to fit the cases of other groups' (1971, p. 29). These 'other groups' would presumably include women as well as children, the unemployed and retired people. This assumption that minor modifications to the model would enable it to account for women's situation has been heavily criticised: 'It is precisely this assumption (that women form a specific offshoot from the male category which is synonymous with the neutral, general category) that constitutes what has been described as masculine hegemony' (Griffin *et al.*, 1982).

Another widely read and influential approach to leisure studies has been characterised by Clarke as 'policy reformist' and within 'a Fabian mould' (Clarke in Tomlinson, 1981). It is perhaps best exemplified by the work of Young and Willmott (1973) and that of the Rapoports (1975). Both texts share an elitist assumption that the tastes and leisure interests of the middle classes will, in the course of time, become available to all – a model of society which assumes a steady flow of historical 'improvement'. This approach tells us nothing about inequalities of gender and race, and offers an inadequate theorisation of class relations and cultures. Major problems with the types of approach outlined above concern both the siting of leisure unproblematically within the family, which is seen as static and isolated from other social structures, and the limitations of the methodologies used.

Marxist approaches

Some other approaches to leisure studies over the last decade have similarly failed to deal adequately with gender issues, albeit for different reasons. Relatively recent Marxist analyses have emphasised the wage relationship as the major determinant of leisure in capitalist society, leisure being as seen as clearly constructed by type and hours of paid work (Stedman-Jones, cited in Tomlinson, 1981). In adopting this perspective on leisure in relation to paid employment, women's experiences are rendered irrelevant, peripheral or merely difficult to study. Whilst men are generally seen to 'earn' leisure time through paid work, the amorphous nature of women's unpaid domestic work as carers makes it hard to identify time that is unambiguously 'free' for leisure. Although the above approach has much to offer and is 'alive and well' (Clarke and Critcher, 1985), in emphasising the negative features of leisure as heavily commercialised and packaged by capitalism, the positive aspects tend to become obscured (Deem, 1986a). Strategies for improving access to leisure are cast as 'reformist' and one-dimensional, for example as compensation for mind-dulling work or unemployment (Carrington and Leaman, 1983). Having said this, the emphasis on class inequalities and cultural patterns is a major improvement on most of the positions discussed above, and there are recent attempts to incorporate the issues of gender and race within this analytic framework.

Most leisure studies in the 1970s failed to develop the theorisation of leisure as a social process that was implicit in earlier community studies and cultural criticism. They emphasised instead the family as an unproblematic arena for increased amounts of home-based leisure. Such a one-dimensional model of the family obscures its operation as a social institution within capitalist society which contributes to the reproduction of class, racial and gender inequalities. This context of patriarchal capitalism is a crucial element in any attempt to explain how social forces shape and constrain individuals' choices about their leisure.

'Bridging the gap': attempts by non-feminists to take account of gender

Feminist critiques of the gender-blindness of traditional perspectives in the sociology of leisure have resulted in uneven attempts by some theorists in the area to take account of gender divisions. Roberts (1978) includes a brief discussion of gender in his analysis of the influence exerted by the family on leisure patterns. He notes (p. 96) that:

> In general leisure time is not evenly distributed between husbands and wives. Women are very much the second class citizens. Inequalities in the distribution of leisure time within families make the contrasts that can be drawn between social classes pale to insignificance.

This is a surprising comment, given that he spends barely six pages discussing gender, in contrast to devoting at least a chapter to issues related to social class. A more curious approach, which makes a token attempt to recognise the differences in men's and women's leisure, is taken in an examination of the major theoretical approaches by Rojek (1985). His reworking of theories of leisure, analysing what he refers to as 'multi-paradigmatic rivalry', includes an equally brief analysis of the case of women's leisure in relation to 'the problem of "free time"'. This examination of women's leisure is used as a form of 'case study' through which to demonstrate the limitations inherent in using the concept of free time as the basis for leisure theory and research. Rojek recognises that women's experience of leisure should be set within 'the basic structural characteristics of leisure relations in capitalist society' (p. 18). Unfortunately he neglects to develop this perspective on women into a consideration of gender relations, despite his obvious familiarity with some of the feminist approaches in the area.

No such incomplete perspectives are to be found in the recent work of Parker, who, in answer to critics of his male-dominated approach and his concentration on the leisure of full-time workers (see, for example, McIntosh, 1981), suggests that women's leisure patterns are only different from men's if they are not involved in paid work outside the home. In this case they can be dealt with in a general chapter on 'the unwaged'. Parker is seemingly unaware that inequalities arising from gender divisions are perhaps at their most extreme among the unwaged. Binns and Mars's (1984) study of the effect of male unemployment on family and community relations demonstrates these inequalities, particularly in relation to the continuingly unequal division of domestic labour. Although male partners, like their wives, spent most of their time in the home, across the two age groups studied the wives of the unemployed men still retained overall responsibility for home management, with the husbands taking on particular jobs of a limited or irregular nature which served to emphasise the temporary nature of the arrangement. As Binns and Mars note (p. 681):

> the assumption that a husband's housework is optional and supplementary to that of his wife trivialises his contribution. From the wife's standpoint it may be more of a hindrance than a help. Permanent financial hardship reinforces and underlines the essential imbalance.

While it is clear the majority of women in this study accepted both formal and practical responsibility for what they referred to as 'home management', in contradiction there was a shared consciousness of increased domestic equality among some of the couples. This mirrors Parker's confidence in the minimal effects of gender divisions, and is evident in the following assertion that:

> Unmarried women (except most of those over pension age) normally have out-of-home jobs and although their leisure behaviour does differ in some ways from those of men, the nature of their work-leisure relationships is not markedly affected by their gender. (Parker, 1983, p. 62)

Parker's most recent position suggests an ignorance of existing evidence which clearly shows that both women's position as paid workers and their access to and experience of leisure, are crucially affected by gender (West, 1982; Deem, 1984). This represents a vital flaw in his argument which is deepened by the following statement from the same text:

> Married women who have full- or part-time jobs may have husbands who share in varying degrees the household and child-rearing tasks: if the husband's share is minimal, then work and leisure lives may approximate to those of unmarried working women. (p. 62)

Contrary to Parker's assumptions, recent research on part-time women workers (Green and Parry, 1982; Sharpe, 1984) is full of interview data which clearly illustrate the opposite. Married women with children and a part-time job are under pressure to conform to the same high standards of housework and childcare as full-time housewives, and in addition to live up to prevailing stereotypes of 'the good worker' when they are in their place of work. This leaves pitifully little time and few opportunities for leisure, as this quote from a Sheffield mother of two illustrates:

> I work two nights a week in a shop and I find it more tiring working the hours I do, than I think I would if I worked in the day, because I work 5 p.m. while 7 p.m. and half past five while one in the morning. I think that's why I don't find much time for leisure because I'm too tired in the day.

The attempts by the non-feminists outlined above to 'bridge the gap' within leisure studies by taking account of gender divisions are disappointing to say the least. However, a more promising perspective is to be found in the recent work of Clarke and Critcher (1985). Unlike the previous approaches discussed, they begin to construct a theoretical analysis which sites gender as a crucial determinant of leisure activity. It is not simply that women have less time and resources for leisure that men do, but, in a more complex way,

> Gender as a social division in leisure . . . redefines time and space for women as compared with men. Women are expected – and come themselves to expect – to participate in those leisure activities defined as

appropriate for women, at those times and in those places compatible with established female roles. (p. 160)

Throughout their examination of the nature of leisure in Britain today Clarke and Critcher attempt to demonstrate the ways in which leisure both reflects social divisions ultimately rooted outside leisure itself and '"realises" them, becoming one of the powerful means by which social divisions receive expression and validation' (p. 161). Despite a surprising lack of engagement with well-known feminist work in the area, their work represents a welcome attempt both to overcome the traditional inadequate treatment of women's leisure in leisure studies, and to contribute to the development of feminist approaches to the study of leisure.

Feminist accounts

Feminist accounts of women's leisure constitute a significant (if still marginal) part of the body of feminist theory and related empirical data that have emerged within the area of social science research over the last ten years or so. Noteworthy characteristics of this work include documentation of the structure of women's lives as a whole, and a commitment to representing their experiences in their own terms (Oakley, 1974; Pollert, 1981; Sharpe, 1984). This has involved a lengthy and at times acrimonious critique by feminists of the limitations of academic androcentric disciplines. Within the humanities and the social sciences, mainstream work was blind to the significance of gender, and shared a tendency to study social life in compartmentalised areas entitled 'work', 'leisure', 'family life' and so on (Leonard Barker and Allen, 1976a, 1976b; Spender, 1981). Feminist studies have demonstrated that a more illuminating approach involves investigating particular aspects of women's experience in relation to the structure of their lives as a whole. The study of everyday life is especially important for the analysis of women's leisure, and the difficulties associated with attempting to compartmentalise periods of time and activities which are experienced as overlapping and interconnected.

The growing literature on gender issues in leisure has its roots in this general critique of male-dominated sociology and forms a response to the implicit sexism of much early work in the sociology of leisure field. Feminist interest in leisure studies and the sociology of sport (Hall, 1978; Theberge, 1981; Hargreaves, 1982) has opened up new areas of analysis associated with the issues and perspectives with which the women's movement has been prominently concerned. Arguably the most important of these has been to identify leisure and sport as political issues, and to make gender inequalities as significant an area for study as class inequalities.

It has long been noted that men and women engage in different kinds of leisure activities (see, for example, the General Household Surveys of 1973 and 1983). Men report themselves to be involved in more leisure activities and to participate more frequently than women, especially in those activities which involve leaving the home unaccompanied, and in particular in all forms of sport. The only leisure pursuits for which women regularly and more frequently leave the house are bingo and cinema and theatre visits. 'Official' explanations of women's low participation rates in activities outside the home have been couched in terms of women being recreationally 'disadvantaged' (Department of the Environment) or 'socially and geographically deprived' (see Talbot, 1979, p. 1). Feminist analyses of leisure reject this perception of women as a neglected group whose problems are capable of resolution through piecemeal changes in social policy. One such policy is a recent Sports Council campaign to promote women's participation in sport which derived from an interpretation of quantitative data about gender differences in participation rates, car ownership and other 'positivistic' data (Stanley, 1980). In its place a political analysis of gender and leisure is emerging which links wider social processes and individual women's experiences:

> The concepts of patriarchy, gender relations and class are thus basic to this analysis: gender and social class provide the central structuring relations in the division of labour in patriarchal society and operate as overarching constraints on all women but mostly with different effects. The aim (of this research) is not merely to describe the circumstances and activities of women's daily lives, but to relate these to the forces that shape their lives, define their options and scope for experience and autonomy. (Wimbush, 1986, p. 12)

Leisure viewed in this way is not just a matter of facilities or institutions: it is an integral part of social relations, informed by and contributing to the social order (Tomlinson, 1981). The differences between men's and women's access to and experiences of leisure are both an expression of the sexual division of labour in capitalist society generally, and a reinforcement of traditional gender stereotypes.

Feminist researchers, among others, have begun to challenge the view that social class is the major division affecting access to and participation in leisure, identifying gender and also race as equally pertinent divisions structuring individual experiences. Women from different class positions may be unequally constrained by income levels and resources, but share common constraints resulting from their subordinate position as women. As noted above, the process of applying critical feminist perspectives to research on leisure generates a healthy suspicion of over-reliance on positivistic methods. These methods, when used in isolation from qualitative techniques, are inadequate in elucidating the meanings attached by respondents to their behaviour (Griffin *et al.*, 1982). Qualitative methods (such as semi-structured or unstructured interviews) can be used to encourage those being studied to 'tell their own stories' (Graham, 1983) and to explain their behaviour in their own terms. A number of ethnographic studies using this approach have provided rich evidence on the leisure experiences of schoolgirls and young working-class women, in addition to revealing the structural absence of girls from most other ethnographic work on youth cultures (McRobbie, 1978; Hobson, 1978; McCabe, 1981, Griffin *et al.*, 1982).

Taken together, these developments represent a real advance in the conceptualisation of women's leisure. Work and leisure are no longer regarded as separate spheres but instead as a complex set of experiences involving degrees of freedom and constraint. When the 'grey' areas between work and play become a major focus of research instead of being tacked on as an afterthought to the main model, it becomes easier to site leisure in context. Women's lack of time and/or access to leisure should not be presented as a social problem to be resolved through specific campaigns or social policies, but constituted instead as one aspect of the gender relations characteristic of patriarchal capitalism.

As argued above, the concept of patriarchy is central to our theoretical analysis, but we are equally concerned to articulate theories of patriarchy within a broad socialist analysis which cites social class, race and ethnicity as equally pertinent factors in analysing leisure in capitalist societies. Socialist-feminists are committed to analysing the intersection of gender and class relations, as well as questions of racism and ethnicity. Relatively recently the issues of nationalism and imperialism have emerged as areas of strong debate for the British Women's Liberation movement, focusing on the theoretical and political implications for feminism and for Marxism (Hamilton and Barrett, 1986).

This material builds on earlier work which explored the ways in which race and ethnicity contribute to the structure of patriarchal relations (Amos and Parmar, 1984; Barrett and McIntosh, 1985; Ramazanoglu, 1986). These explorations recognise the complexity of such issues and the deep-rooted nature of the structural divisions between women – based on class and ethnic differences of culture, religion and family histories, for example – which generate barriers to the establishment of our common ground as feminists and women. Part of the problem involved in attempts to make the experiences of black women more visible, as a prerequisite for the analysis of the similarities and differences between their structural position and experiences, in comparison with those of white women, concerns the paucity of empirical material available to us as white feminists. Although accounts of black women's lives written in their own terms are growing in number (Wilton, 1978; Davis, 1981; Hooks, 1982; Griffin *et al.*, 1982; Bryan, Dadze and Scafe, 1985), we are still faced with the problem of attempting to theorise a common position as women without misrepresenting our black sisters or minimising the effects of racial difference. The lack of written material on black women's leisure underlines the point about the limited accounts available on the leisure of women generally, and supports our original thesis that the traditional concept of leisure is meaningless when applied to women in general (Green and Woodward, 1986). At the present time we are restricted to the information provided by accounts of black women's lives produced for other purposes. (We will return to this issue in Chapter 4).

Added to this, as feminists we have recently recognised the necessity of changing our research methodologies to enable us to identify the diversity of black women's experiences, as well as considering our potential common basis of oppression. Progress in these areas is slow, but an understanding of our differences as feminists and women will hopefully lay the ground for a parallel understanding of the historical and political factors that have exacerbated and exaggerated those differences.

Developing our own perspective

The small amount of empirical data available on women's leisure, whether collected indirectly as part of other projects (for example, Hobson, 1978; Hunt, 1980; Finch and Groves, 1983) or more directly, as the focus of a study (Talbot, 1979; Deem, 1982, 1986; Wimbush, 1986), tends to be qualitative in nature, and in the case of the former three studies, centred upon leisure in the domestic sphere. Whilst this is obviously an important focus, as Deem (1984, p. 3) argues,

> if other influences are missed or minimised, then important aspects of women's lives and of the social and economic structures which determine women's lives may be ignored.

From the inception of the Sheffield project we were convinced of the need for the broadest possible examination of the divisions and differences between women, taking due account of variations in their social background, in order to avoid lumping women together as a 'women and leisure' problem, in the fashion of traditional leisure studies. The obvious structural factors in question are divisions of social class and associated cultures, which affect the nature of employment and access to independent income for women, as well as their command of material resources and levels of education attained. Additional factors, also structural in nature but not always so obvious to analysts, are crucial in terms of their implications for women's leisure time and activities: differences of age, household composition (including the presence of a partner), number and ages of children, sexual orientation, and the work and leisure pursuits of friends, children, lovers and husbands. These factors, together with women's own perceptions of appropriate leisure time and activities, are central to any analysis of the constraints on women's leisure.

'The need for a combination of research methods'

Although feminists have been critical of traditional research in the social sciences, particularly that which relies heavily on 'counting and measuring techniques' (Oakley, 1974; Roberts, 1981), we chose to utilise for part of the Sheffield study the quantitative technique of the social survey. There were two major reasons behind this choice: first, its merits of enabling greater generalisation of the findings, and, second, the political importance of the 'hard data' collected by surveys in terms of the study's scope for influencing policy decisions. As feminists our primary concern is both to understand the patriarchal structures that oppress women and to seek to change them. In this cause we need to utilise the strengths of quantitative evidence and, as Jayaratne (1983, p. 159) states,

> if some of the traditional procedures used to produce the needed evidence are contrary to our feminist values, then we must change those procedures accordingly.

No social researchers can reliably claim that quantitative data are either truly objective or that they have measured 'reality', given the problems of defining reality. However, 'good' quantitative data, which meet 'accepted standards of validity' – that is, data collected and analysed according to generally accepted procedural methods based on mathematical principles – can be claimed to be more objective than small-scale qualitative data, and therefore to provide evidence with a wider application to the population. In addition, quantitative social science research is often interpreted by the funding bodies and the public as 'the truth', most people being interested in the content of statistics rather than the method by which they are compiled. Generalised statements can provide essential information to influence policy-making bodies in areas where a more informed provision of leisure resources for women could lessen some of the constraints they experience. Survey data on the reasons behind women's low participation rates could also be instrumental in challenging the current virtual monopoly held by men in terms of the content and practice of organised leisure pursuits, in both the public and private sectors. However, the main strength of quantitative data, namely its level of generalisability, presents problems when it comes to the interpretation of perceptual responses in an interview. The collection of this type of data about women's lives requires a more sensitive research technique.

It was to the strengths of qualitative data that we turned in order to understand the complex issues involved in exploring women's leisure experiences as women themselves perceive them. One important issue which surveys are poorly equipped to examine is the fragmentation of women's time, an important factor affecting leisure time and pursuits. This is best explained conceptually by examining the social context in which the majority of women's leisure occurs: the home. As Gregory (1982) and Glyptis and Chambers (1982) argue, the home is an important base for women's leisure, but it is also the space where the most demands (often competing) are made on their time by partners and children. Where no clear boundaries exist between work and leisure, women frequently sacrifice personal leisure in order to accommodate caring for the family, in which case their own time spaces for uninterrupted leisure become fragmented, with the attendant reduced options on how and where to spend it.

Survey data can provide evidence of the nature and extent of structural constraints such as the demands of domestic labour and childcare, usually combined with paid work, which lead to a fragmented working day for women. However, in order to understand fully the forms of leisure then available to women and the ways in which they are facilitated, researchers need to employ alternative techniques, for example engaging in unstructured discussions with women, preferably within an appropriate social context. Conducting interviews with women in their homes, when they are subject to the demands of children and partners, provides researchers with a clear example of both the nature of those demands on women's time and their effects upon concentration.

Leisure for Sheffield women

The aims and conclusions of the Sheffield-based project on leisure and gender are discussed throughout the book. Some of the findings are presented in detail in Chapter 4, but for those readers not familiar with research in this area it is probably helpful to provide a short summary, as a backcloth to the subsequent discussions.

The project was designed to discover more about women's experiences of leisure in everyday life. In the early stages we recognised the importance of collecting both general information pertaining to all women, and more detailed knowledge about different perceptions of and attitudes towards women's leisure. In the summer of 1984 we commissioned National Opinion Polls Ltd to carry out a survey in Sheffield which resulted in interviews with 707 women aged between 18 and 59. They were drawn from randomly selected areas around the city and from a range of social class backgrounds and family situations. A team of interviewers asked the women over a hundred questions covering issues such as their understanding of 'leisure time', their access to and experiences of free time, and how this was restricted, and also a variety of other questions about their lives. The findings from the survey confirmed that women's access to free time and leisure opportunities are structured by social class and income level, age and ethnic group, and their work and domestic situation. The main constraints took the form of a lack of resources such as time, money, safe transport and childcare. Limitations on their access to leisure were experienced most acutely by the women not currently in paid work, those with unemployed partners, single parents, and married women with children aged under five. The leisure activities in which women did engage were also influenced by the constraints outlined above. The results for home-based leisure showed that 95 per cent of respondents watched television, 75 per cent did reading, and 50 per cent did sewing, knitting and crafts, whereas only 23 per cent played sport or went to night clubs and discos. Inexpensive, home-based pursuits were the most popular activities, and those which involved safe transport, independent outings and high costs were the most difficult to sustain.

Anxious to explore the meaning behind these leisure patterns, we set up a series of discussion groups and in-depth interviews with selected groups of women from the survey and their male partners. The most interesting, and in some cases unexpected, findings that emerged out of this stage of the research were concerned with the area commonly termed their 'private lives'. Taking time for themselves was problematic for all the women and heavily influenced by negotiations with partners, children and relatives, as well as their own desire to give priority to satisfying the 'needs' of those close to them. Going out for 'a laugh with the girls' was seen as a leisure highlight, but usually involved careful planning and negotiation, particularly if it included evening drinks at the pub and ending up in a night club. Fear of walking alone after dark and the weight of male partners' disapproval of such activities are reflected in the small percentage of women who reported doing them as a regular activity. (Exploration of these issues is to be found in the chapters that follow.)

The main conclusions drawn from the research report provide a firm empirical base for the book. These are as follows: women generally have less time available for leisure than men and make choices about how to spend their time from a more limited range of possibilities. Women's housework and childcare responsibilities do not fit neatly into a conventional working day, and many women are almost constantly 'on call', which makes it difficult to plan leisure in advance with any degree of certainty. Making arrangements to spend leisure time outside the home is particularly problematic, resulting in most so-called free time being spent in the home. Women are generally financially poorer than men, with most married women still being financially dependent on their husbands. Women's leisure is given low priority in household budgets, with men's right to personal spending money more widely accepted. Finally, many groups of women are expected to choose their leisure time activities mainly from within the limited range of home and family-oriented activities which are socially defined as acceptable, womanly pursuits.

This chapter has introduced the central issues raised by an analysis of women's leisure. Within a review of attempts to define leisure, we combine a critique of traditional concepts with an analysis of more recent contributions to the debate. Having engaged in a brief discussion of the dominant perspectives in the field of leisure studies and the sociology of leisure, we trace the emergence of feminist perspectives, detailing both their critique of androcentric approaches and the alternatives proposed. Finally, we outline our own approach drawing in detail on the Sheffield study to highlight the need to use a range of research methods, and to summarise the resulting empirical data.

Within the broad framework of socialist feminism we focus on the issue of structural constraints which contribute to the social control of women's free time and their access to opportunities and resources for leisure. This concept of social control locates it within the historically constituted structures, processes and divisions characteristic of contemporary capitalism. Viewed in this way, social control operates at a number of levels across what may be seen as a continuum (Green, Hebron and Woodward, 1987c) ranging from non-coercive forms to actual physical violence. In addition, such forms of control are closely related to ideologies of gender and gender-appropriate behaviour, one of the issues addressed in detail in the next chapter.

2

Capitalism, patriarchy and ideologies of leisure

Introduction

This chapter builds on the theoretical premises outlined in the previous chapter and attempts to move towards an understanding of leisure from a socialist feminist perspective. It is informed by theoretical writings in the area of cultural studies rather than by more conventional work in leisure studies. We find the critical approach to the analysis of cultural forms which is characteristic of British cultural studies to be useful in highlighting the problematic nature of our taken-for-granted assumptions about leisure.

It will be clear by now that we take issue with the notion that leisure is an area of unlimited free choice, and that a better understanding recognises that it is significantly determined by the broader economic and political context. We need to examine the characteristics of capitalist relations of production, and how leisure is shaped by them. In 'relations of production' we include not only class relations and class struggles, but also those of gender and race (Barrett, 1985). Throughout this chapter we will be arguing that the relationship between the economic organisation of a society and the nature of leisure is not a straightforward, one-way determination but a more complex, and to some extent reciprocal, process. We shall be examining the importance of ideology and hegemonic struggle in the maintenance and reproduction of inequalities in leisure.

Culture, hegemony, ideology

Some of the more exciting interventions into the 'leisure studies' field in the last few years have been those which seek to develop the links between the analysis of culture and the study of leisure. Such attempts to break down unhelpful barriers are to be welcomed, specifically for their efforts to problematise the very concept of leisure itself. Much of this work is relatively new, and offers suggestions for new directions, rather than solutions to enduring problems. For instance, cultural studies has a substantial history of debate over definitions of culture. In our own attempts to theorise leisure we have at times been preoccupied with questions about the relationship of 'leisure' to 'culture'. If we hope to examine leisure as a part of culture, then it is clear that we cannot adopt a narrow definition of culture centred on 'high' cultural products or texts. To do so would involve conceptualising culture as specific elements or forms of leisure rather than vice versa. More useful for our purpose is the definition of culture by Raymond Williams (1961) as a 'whole way of life', taking on board Hall's (1981) comment that this is an over-simplification. Hall argues (p. 22) that the theory of culture involves 'The study of relationships between elements in the whole way of life . . . , culture is threaded through all social practices, and is the sum of their relationship.' Perhaps, then, by attempting to study leisure we are abstracting certain social practices from the broader framework which is culture. Some forms of leisure, most notably the reading of magazines, and popular literature, film and television, have been examined within cultural studies. The broad range of cultural forms that have been examined might be taken as showing that cultural studies is best defined by its critical approach. This is not to deny that within cultural studies there has also been debate (usually healthy) and dissent about approach, rooted in the debates between the often overly polarised 'culturalist' and 'structuralist' traditions. Readers who are interested in this can follow the discussion in Johnson (1979) and Hall (1981). For us, the main value of what might be defined as the cultural studies approach, as developed in the work of the Centre for Contemporary Cultural Studies at Birmingham University, has been the reworking and mobilisation of key theoretical concepts, as outlined below. What we have found most useful has been the broad framework, which involves 'a way of looking critically at innocent practices;

practices that seem not to be implicated, that is, in politics and power,' (Johnson, 1987, p. 207).

Leisure, more than many other social practices, has been constructed as 'innocent'. Indeed, the tendency is to contrast leisure with those areas of life where politics and power do impinge, most notably the public domain of paid work. However, even a cursory glance at historical and contemporary experiences of leisure reveal, not surprisingly perhaps, that leisure has not escaped the intervention of either power or politics.

Clearly, we live our lives in circumstances which are characterised by obvious inequalities. More than this, we are actively involved in the reproduction of society and its inequalities. Not only is leisure divided along lines of class, race, gender, age and sexual orientation, and more, but leisure must also be seen as an area of life where these divisions are negotiated, redefined or reproduced. Our primary concern is to understand the relationship between leisure, both conceptually and experientially, and the maintenance of inequality between men and women. One starting point for this is in an examination of the concept of hegemony. Although the term has enjoyed currency for some time in leisure studies (see, for example, the papers in Tomlinson, 1981), it has so far made little impact on the counting and measuring world of mainstream leisure research.

Hegemony refers to the process by which dominant groups win consent to their domination. Although originally developed by Gramsci in the context of unequal class relations, it is also relevant to a consideration of the dominance of men over women. Gramsci used hegemony as an analytic category to examine

> the precise political cultural and ideological forms through which, in any given society, a fundamental class is able to establish its leadership as distinct from more coercive forms of domination. (Bennett, 1981, p. 187)

As Hall (1977) has pointed out, hegemony depends upon both force and consent, but for Gramsci in 'the liberal capitalist state' consent is usually in the lead, operating behind 'the armour of coercion'. What this means for women is that not only do they generally share a subordinate economic and social position, but the hegemonic process works to ensure that male domination is seen as legitimate. This legitimation is a continual process: hegemony is never won, once and for all, but involves a continuing struggle. This struggle takes place within social institutions such as the education system, the family and the media, as well as through the more repressive agencies such as the legal system, the police, and so on. Although not specifically a cultural institution, we argue that leisure is also a site of hegemonic struggle.

One important consideration is the fact that because hegemony is won through struggle, it can also be lost. In terms of upholding the status quo, it is generally argued that the winning of consent is more effective than domination through coercion or repression. This is important when we come to look at gender. How is consent won? Why is it that women can sometimes be said to collude in their own oppression? In order to account for this we need to take account of the role of ideology. By ideology, we understand the complex system of perceptions and representations through which we experience ourselves and come to make sense of the world. Our own perspective is closest to that of Barrett (1980), who states that whilst ideology exists in and through material apparatuses, such as schools or the media, and in their practices, it does not automatically follow that ideology is itself material. Ideology is 'a generic term for the process by which meaning is produced, challenged, re-produced, trans-formed' (Barrett, 1980). Ideology is a process which is neither completely determined by the relations of production nor completely autonomous from them. Rather, it is relatively autonomous; that is, ideological representations are related to social reality, but are also shaped by the system of representation through which they are articulated. So, for instance, if one thinks of specific ideologies, such as the ideology of motherhood, the nature of the representation will have a bearing on the particular version of motherhood that is being presented. There may be commonalities between different representations, but they will not be straightfor-ward reproductions of existing social relations. They will be mediated versions of reality, and the medium or signifying system will shape how an ideological message is presented and to some extent how it is read.

Ideology is crucial in the struggle for hegemony. In his definition of ideology Eagleton (1976) characterises it as a process whereby 'the situation in which one social class has power over the other is either seen by most members of society as 'natural' or not seen at all'. Ideology serves to conceal contradictions and antagonisms, rendering them invisible or else seemingly a normal part of the given social order. This applies as much, if not more, to antagonisms around gender and race as to class antagonisms. So women's unequal position in society is in turn not seen, or is seen as natural, given, immutable.

We are interested in how ideologies of gender structure leisure, bearing in mind the fact that gender ideologies are cut across by class, race and other divisions. We are concerned with the way in which leisure as a category of experience is itself gendered, the way in which leisure is, in Johnson's (1987, p. 214) terms, 'a grossly ideological category based firmly on a male and relatively affluent experience'.

In discussing ideology we do not wish to imply that all women are identical recipients of a dominant ideology imposed from above (see also Perkins, 1979). Indeed, rather than subscribing to the notion that there is a coherent dominant ideology, we find Hall's (1977) concept of ideological work illuminating in this context, in terms of his theorisation of how ideology works to win consent for preferred interpretations or definitions. In a society where those who control the 'means of material production' are also likely to control the 'means of mental production' (and Hall is specifically concerned with the mass media) we are likely to be offered a range of representations which fall within a dominant framework whilst offering an apparent plurality. A relevant area where this has been developed is in the study of girls' and women's magazines (McRobbie, 1982; Winship, 1978). Studies such as these show the narrow definitions of femininity that are offered in the mainstream media.

A woman's place

Our own research has shown that leisure is clearly structured through gender. We have already noted how the prevailing definition of leisure is one which characterises it as time free from the obligations of paid work and how this definition is inappropriate for the majority of women (and for increasing numbers of men). This division has been historically constructed, as we illustrate in Chapter 3. It has its roots in the ideology of gender, which

> has played an important part in the historical construction of the capitalist division of labour and in the reproduction of labour power. A

sexual division of labour and accompanying ideologies of the appropriate meaning of labour for men and women have been embedded in the capitalist division of labour from its beginnings. (Barrett, 1985, p. 74)

However, the sexual division of labour does not only have an accompanying gendered ideology of labour, but also involves an ideology about the appropriate meanings of leisure for men and for women.

Historical studies have illustrated the way in which gender inequalities pre-dated capitalism. Dobash and Dobash (1980) give examples of the commodification of women during the medieval period, whereby women were status symbols of the power of men. The concept of patriarchy is central to our analysis of gender relations, although we do not find the concept entirely unproblematic (see also Rowbotham, 1979; Hearn, 1987). Most literally meaning 'power of the father', we are using the term in its broader sense to refer to a system of social relations characterised by male domination over women. As a system of family organisation it was the norm in pre-capitalist Britain. However, capitalism developed and utilised the distinctions between male and female areas of activities. Men's primary role was in production, whereas women's was in the necessary reproduction of the labour force. Of course, women have always been involved in the productive process too, depending upon their particular position in the class hierarchy and on specific historical circumstances. Despite this, the dominant ideological distinction between women and men is rooted in the reproduction/production relationship.

In our day-to-day lives we encounter a vast array of information, from commonsense assumptions and norms, through to books, films, television and other cultural products, which present particular versions of what it is to be a woman. These frequently present only parts of women's experiences, which stand for the whole. Ideology works at the point of representation and shows to us real women what 'real women' are like. In theory we all draw upon the particular range of femininities on offer to make sense (or not) of our lives. Gender ideology is rooted in and builds on the biological distinction of sex. Women's reproductive capacity becomes the basis for definitions of what constitutes 'femininity' as opposed to 'masculinity'. A recourse to biology has been used historically to offer a general definition of women as inferior, but it has also been mobilised to render particular activities, such as most sport, unsuitable for women because of the potential damage to their reproductive organs. (In fact, as recent work by Blue, 1987, has pointed out, it is male genitalia that are substantially more at risk than women's.) Although the social construct of 'femininity' does vary to some degree depending on historical conditions, it seems fair to say that current definitions are not substantially different from those that prevailed in the nineteenth century.

Fundamentally, femininity hinges on maternity and domesticity. It interacts with a particular ideology of the family and incorporates an ideology of romantic heterosexual love. Femininity implies a preoccupation with the private, the personal. If masculinity is strength, superiority, domination, rationality, then femininity is weakness, inferiority, submission, irrationality. Women gain their identities through their relationships with men: they are wives, mothers and daughters. This applies not only to women who fall into these categories, but also to women who do not, who are identified as not-wives and not-mothers. Women who do not have the status of being attached to a man or men are generally treated with pity; this is not a situation, it is assumed, that one would actually choose.

These assumptions have important implications for leisure. First, even when women do engage in paid work, this is typically seen as secondary to their work within the household or family, so women are not seen to 'earn' the right to leisure in the same way as men. Second, because domesticity and maternity are presented as the source of women's pleasure, we are not supposed to need to seek personal gratification from leisure, and to do so is considered selfish. Representations of family life typically show wives and mothers in servicing roles. From an early age women learn to moderate our own needs, desires and wishes to those of other people. This applies in leisure as in other areas, so that much of so-called family leisure actually involves women as hidden workers, be it washing sports kit, ferrying children to activities, or just generally being on call and available.

Given the emphasis on family leisure and indeed on the institution of 'the family' generally in the current political climate, we would be foolish to underestimate its importance. The majority of the British population live within a family grouping, although recent figures confirm that only three households in ten are married couples with dependent children (Family Policy Studies Centre, 1985). As Clarke and Critcher (1985, p. 44) point out,

> Members of the family socialise each other into sex roles. These cannot exist without the family and are continuously reproduced within it. But they also exist outside it, in the organisation of the economy and the prevailing ideologies of sexuality.

It is to the second of these considerations that we now turn, to look at the implications for leisure of the way in which female sexuality has been defined, constructed and controlled.

Commonsense ideas about female sexuality typically divide women into two main categories: angels and whores. This is not to deny that these categories are refined and subdivided into a wider typography, but the basic distinction is between good, respectable, heterosexual women, and immoral, promiscuous, heterosexual women. Women who are not heterosexual are still likely to be seen as abnormal or abhorrent or else are ignored completely. Just about the only condition under which female sexuality can be legitimately expressed is that of monogamous heterosexuality.

Within such relationships, most typically of course marriage, there has been a long history of the social control of women by men, tied in with the notion that women were the property of their husbands. Dobash and Dobash (1980) chronicle the way in which husbands have been legally allowed, and were even expected by other men, to chastise wives who were failing in their wifely duties. This went hand in hand with a double standard of morality, which required wives to be respectable and circumspect in their behaviour. Wives who did not conform to this model of behaviour were liable to be punished by husbands. It seems almost amazing that ideas about female respectability and appropriate behaviour which have their roots hundreds of years in the past should have a direct impact on women's leisure today, but as we go on to illustrate in more detail in Chapter 6, this is clearly the case. The social control of men over women at an individual level is a part and parcel of everyday life for most women, whether this control comes from their own partners, or family members, or others. What is more, women are also subject to social control on a wider scale, as we have discussed elsewhere (Green, Hebron and Woodward, 1987b; Green and Woodward, 1988). Women's leisure outside the home is often 'policed' by the actions of men, or by women's own expectations, such as their fear of male violence.

Debates about social control within the area of leisure studies have tended to focus on the attempts of the middle classes to impose their will on the working class, and have largely been preoccupied with male work and leisure experiences. Our own focus on the notion of social control is informed more by feminist work on the areas of sexuality and violence against women (Smart and Smart, 1978; Hanmer and Maynard, 1987). We understand the processes of social control as vital to an analysis of the maintenance of masculine hegemony. If we are talking about the relative importance of 'consent' as opposed to 'coercion', then we should take account of the fact that when individual women fail to consent to their own subordination, they may face the ultimate threat of male violence. It is worth noting that such behaviour on the part of men is not unusual or abnormal. It is, as Wilson (1983) has commented, a rather unfortunate and extreme version of 'normal' masculine behaviour.

Leisure

The extent to which leisure is structured through an ideology of gender highlights how the concept can itself be seen as an ideological category. We all hold particular beliefs of what leisure is. We bring this understanding to our experiences of leisure, and in turn our understanding is shaped by these experiences. One important element in this process is the extent to which our experiences fit with our perceptions of what leisure ought to be. As Johnson (1987, p. 214) observes, leisure is a prime example of the way in which 'the meanings of terms are extended in democratic or egalitarian directions whilst actual inequalities remain', so that whilst leisure is an area of apparent (and to some extent) actual choice and plurality, some definitions of leisure carry more weight than others. Johnson gives the example of the rhetoric of self-improvement or betterment which informs much contemporary thinking about leisure management. The fact that leisure has developed historically as an area which needs to be 'managed' at all, and in these directions in particular, is discussed in Chapter 3.

Aside from this example, we can extend Johnson's argument to encompass some of the most fundamental common assumptions about the characteristics of leisure. In this way, the construction of leisure as time free from obligations to be spent as each individual chooses is rendered transparent, and we see that this is a definition which fits the social reality of the minority rather than the majority of people. As Johnson acknowledges, for some groups leisure in these terms is not a social reality at all. It is not very surprising, then, that many of the women we talked to about their leisure responded initially by telling us that they did not have any leisure at all.

In her discussion of sport, Hargreaves (1982a) points out that it is not enough to see sport in terms of how it is related to 'modes of production, the state, education, the media, the family, ethnic groups and other cultural practices'. Though this is important, we also need to understand the extent to which, and in what ways, sport is involved in the mediation of ideas and beliefs. We would certainly make the same point about leisure more generally. However, because leisure as a cultural category encompasses such a diversity of forms and meanings, it may be that we should reconsider the extent to which it is possible to treat leisure as a monolithic category. Perhaps the point we feel is most important, and it is one worth making despite the difficulties with the concept of leisure, is that the experiences we think of as leisure do involve processes whereby ideas and beliefs are mediated. This is most obvious in the sense that it is precisely in our leisure time that we engage with the cultural forms which deal with representation and the production of meaning; we read, we watch television, we listen to the radio, some of us watch films, plays, and so on. We also engage in social interaction. We actively construct meanings which help us to make sense of our lives, and of society more generally. Much of this construction takes place in our leisure time. These are the most obvious examples, perhaps, but not the only ones. Across the range of experiences which we might think of as leisure we are actively involved with the production of meaning, whether we are reproducing the status quo or challenging it.

Conclusion

An adequate understanding of leisure needs to situate it in its social context – in our case within a social organisation that is fundamentally patriarchal and fundamentally capitalist. An important area of study which offers a useful critical framework for theorising leisure is that of cultural studies. This has informed our use of the concept of hegemony as central to our own analysis. By hegemony, we understand the process of struggle to win consent to the domination of one group over others. This helps us to look at how it is that leisure is not only an area where social divisions structure access and experience, but is also an area where inequalities are negotiated, reproduced and challenged. Ideology plays an important part in the struggle to win consent. Leisure is defined through ideologies of masculinity and femininity, through ideas about appropriate male and female roles, concerns and behaviour. Ideologies of class and race also bear upon our social definitions of leisure. We can see leisure itself as an ideological category in the extent to which it is understood in commonsense terms to be neutral, in the sense of being free from the influences of power and politics. Our own findings about gender inequalities in leisure indicate that this is patently not the case.

3

A social history of women's leisure

A historical perspective is essential for those of us who are interested in exploring and understanding women's lives, given that leisure does not exist in a vacuum, but is shaped by the broader social context. As Rojek (1985), among others, has pointed out, leisure should be seen as a part of dynamic relations which change over time. It comes as little surprise, then, to find that the social and economic changes that have taken place in Britain from the eighteenth century on have had clear implications for the way in which leisure is currently shaped and perceived. This applies not only to the leisure 'choices' that are possible in terms of the kind of provision and the material resources available to individuals or groups, but also to our broader definitions of leisure and our ideas about what leisure is, or ought to be.

As with many other areas of women's lives, uncovering a social history of women's leisure is no easy task. Though there is a growing body of feminist writing which aims to uncover the history of women's paid employment and domestic labour, there has been little comparable literature about leisure. In addition, though there is a good deal of historical material on leisure now available, this rarely tells us much about women's experiences. As Clarke and Critcher (1985) comment, the specific focus of much of this work on institutionalised forms of leisure means that 'the history of leisure is predominantly a history of male leisure'. We might assume that in the past, as now, relatively few women were taking part in organised and visible leisure activities. Then, as now, women's leisure did not typically exist as discrete periods of time passed in public places. This explains in part why women appear so little in histories of leisure. To this we should add that, as Chapter 1 indicated, leisure studies is no different from other disciplines where, until recently, men's experiences were treated as the norm and the omission of data about women was not entirely accidental.

Fortunately, it is possible to discover something about how women experienced leisure in the past by turning to a range of other material. We will be suggesting some possibilities, though we by no means claim to have carried out the task of providing a comprehensive list of sources. Nor are we supplying a complete chronicle of the social history of women's leisure. Feminists working in this area are inevitably placed in a position of having to sift through a wide variety of material in order to pick out a few relevant points. However, given that we are committed to studying leisure in the wider context of women's lives as a whole, we have found some existing studies extremely useful. These have been studies which either attempt to describe and explain the whole of women's lives in particular historical (and sometimes economic and geographical) locations, or which emphasise one particular aspect of women's lives such as employment or family experience, whilst taking account of the wider historical and social context. Examples of this kind of work are Diana Gittins's *Fair Sex* (1982) and Elizabeth Roberts's *A Woman's Place* (1984), both of which provide useful and interesting insights into the leisure experiences of earlier generations of women.

Another route into uncovering women's leisure experiences is the 're-reading' of texts which are not primarily about either leisure or women's experience. Although in some cases we might disagree with their orientation or interpretation, they can provide useful descriptive material. Coalter and Parry (1982) have noted the relevance of the various 'community studies' such as *Coal Is our Life* (Dennis, Henriques and Slaughter, 1969) and *Middletown* (Lynd and Lynd, 1929). Though community studies have been criticised for their lack of generalisable data and their failure to look at influential factors beyond the level of the immediate community, their strength for us lies in their attempts to look across different areas of life, including family relations and social networks. For this reason, we have used them here for their historical interest, and will also be returning to them briefly in Chapter 5.

However, even drawing on such a range of sources, there are obvious omissions. One significant omission is the lack of material on the history of black women's experiences. Just as women's history has only recently started to be written, similarly the history of black people in Britain has largely been suppressed or ignored. (We return to this issue in Chapter 4).

The following discussion is largely ethnocentric in that it refers almost exclusively to white British experience. Furthermore, even among white Britons there have always been differences between regions, and certainly between countries, which make it difficult to present a straightforward summary of the impact of social and economic changes on leisure during the last two hundred years. Despite this, and despite the restrictions imposed by focusing only on Britain, we hope that some of the points raised will facilitate comparison with other Western industralised capitalist nations.

Industrialisation and leisure

Among those working in the leisure field there is an apparent consensus about the key historical periods. While the precise dates may vary, the majority take as their starting point the Industrial Revolution. (Rojek, 1985, is one notable exception, arguing that in fact we need to go back and study medieval times). Indeed, some of the most interesting historical work on leisure has been concerned with the impact of industrialisation. Leisure is not usually the primary focus of such work but is looked at in terms of its relationship with paid work (see, for instance, Thompson, 1968; Hobsbawm, 1960). The changing nature of employment is fundamental to the development of our understanding of leisure. However, the preoccupation with class, important in itself, does mean that relatively little attention is paid to the different experiences of men and women. In fact it seems either to be implicitly assumed that all workers are male, or else little concession is made to the fact that the experiences of women workers were not (and are not) identical to those of men.

We would certainly agree that 'The Industrial Revolution marks the most fundamental transformation of human life in the history of the world recorded in written documents'. (Hobsbawm, 1960, p. 13).

This 'fundamental transformation' involved for many the radical restructuring of time, together with the separation of home and workplace. Numerous commentators have contrasted the nature of people's lives in pre-industrial society, where boundaries between work and leisure were blurred, with the more highly organised division in time and space brought by industrialisation. This does not mean that the changes were always straightforward or smoothly effected. There is evidence of resistance to these changes: for example, workers' persistence in taking Monday as a holiday (Saint Monday) was a source of irritation to many of the new industrialists (Reid, 1986) who finally sought to combat this by introducing the Saturday half-day. By and large, however, the late eighteenth and early nineteenth centuries saw continuing change, in particular the consolidation of the division between work and leisure. Attempts were made to 'tame' the workforce, attempts which spread beyond working hours and into leisure time (Clarke and Critcher, 1985). These centred on the need to 'encourage' good timekeeping, sobriety, and so on.

Clearly, not everyone experienced these changes in the same way. Rowbotham (1973) has pointed out the differences between working-class and middle-class women. She argues that by the early nineteenth century the middle class were for the first time beginning to see themselves as a class. Whilst middle-class men gained status from their own industry, this was not true for their wives. For them it was their leisure that was seen as further proof of the husband's status. Women in the emergent middle class withdrew first from labour outside the home, then from work within it. Their daughters began to be educated for leisure: 'The girls learned accomplishments, the boys received an academic education' (Rowbotham, 1973, p. 23). Rowbotham goes on to state that by the late 1800s,

> Although the circumstances of middle class women improved with the growing power in society of their men, their relationship was one of increasing economic dependence. In this sense patriarchy was strengthened. The women were part of the men's belongings, their leisure, the sign of his conspicuous consumption' (p. 47)

In their discussion of the 1840s, Clarke and Critcher develop the argument that it was in this period that leisure emerged as a discrete area separate from work: 'This antithesis of work and leisure (from which so many contemporary accounts begin) is not a given social fact, but an historical creation' (Clarke and Critcher, 1985, p. 58).

Given that at this time factory workers were working a six-day, seventy-hour week, it should be pointed out that opportunities for leisure were limited. By the mid nineteenth century the majority of the British population lived in towns and cities. Increasing urbanisation contributed to the shape of leisure. For most people 'life was now dominated by the place and pace of work' (Walvin, 1978). Workers not only lacked time for recreation, they also lacked facilities, including open spaces. We can speculate that the lack of time was likely to be particularly acute for women working both inside and outside the home. Similarly, what Walvin identifies as the two major leisure pursuits during this period – organised drinking and prostitution – offered little scope for women:

> both drink and commercial sex catered primarily for the pleasures of men . . . Women had in general to create a recreational world from within the limitations of family life. (Walvin, 1978, p. 46)

In practice the two recreations were often strongly associated with and centred on that bastion of masculine culture, the public house. As Valerie Hey (1986) points out, the link between prostitution and drinking is a legacy which still affects women's access to pubs today. The nature of public houses, the reality of women's responsibilities for home and childcare, and the dominant ideologies of feminine respectability and morality combined to ensure that when women did drink alcohol this was more likely to be done in the relative privacy of their homes or stair-head drinking clubs than in pubs.

This leads us to consider the important differences in the role of the home for middle- and working-class families. For middle-class men, the home was increasingly portrayed as the site of much of their leisure. Working-class men, in the main, sought leisure outside the home, which was likely to be cramped and overcrowded. For both working-class and middle-class women, escape from the home in search of leisure was not a realistic proposition. Rather, the Victorian era saw the development of the home represented as a haven, the place to which men returned tired at the end of the day's toil. The role of the wife was the angel in the house: virtuous, respectable and concerned to provide comfort and succour to her husband. It is difficult to gauge how accurately this sums up middle-class life by the mid 1800s. It was, and in fact continues to be, a pervasive ideology. However, for working-class women, this rosy if restricted vision bore little resemblance to their own experience of almost relentless work, paid and unpaid.

Industrialists were often initially keen to employ women (and children), seeing them as more easy to discipline than men. However, one employer commented: 'We can get the lads on Monday, but not the women and girls who are more "giddy" ' (quoted in Reid, 1986, p. 109). As the author points out:

> For wives and such, 'giddiness' was in fact very sensible if their wage only supplemented the family income and they needed the Monday to perform domestic tasks.

This provides a telling example of how many working-class women spent their so-called 'free time' outside paid employment.

Apart from the considerable changes wrought by industrialisation in terms of the amount and organisation of time available for leisure, there were obviously changes in the ways in which such time was spent. For the working class in particular a tightened control over their working hours overlapped to some extent into non-working hours. The possibilities for pre-industrial pastimes were eroded, and the drive for 'rational recreation' began.

An illuminating discussion of the process of rational recreation can be found in Cunningham (1980). However, Cunningham concentrates almost exclusively on class relations to the exclusion of gender relations. We would agree with his contention that whilst rational recreation was 'a crude attempt at social control' to impose middle-class values on the working class, it cannot be reduced to just this. It was also motivated in part by a drive

> to open up to the working class cultural and aesthetic experiences from which it had been previously excluded. Books, museums, exhibitions, music, all these cultural goods from the middle-class repertoire were in a sense to be laid at the feet of a presumably grateful working class. (Cunningham, 1980, p. 91)

Working-class leisure was seen by some members of the middle class as a problem, which they perceived could be solved by expanding their own 'rational recreational ideas'. Of course, this essentially patronising and reformist approach was not always welcome. Early initiatives were developed through the Church or through organisations such as mechanics institutes or temperance societies, and the paternalist model was taken up by local authorities when they began to levy a rate for some leisure provision, notably parks, libraries, baths and museums. As a philosophy it has been remarkably persistent, and remnants of it are still with us today.

It is difficult to assess the impact of these early developments for women. The 'problem' of working-class leisure was seen mainly in terms of its emphasis on drink and sexual licence. Therefore it seems that the implicit concern of middle-class reformers was with the male working class. Women were less likely to engage in rowdy or drunken behaviour in public spaces, and therefore were presumably not seen as a problem. As Clarke and Critcher (1985) have pointed out, whilst working-class men were encouraged towards rational recreation, working-class women were inculcated in the ways of 'rational domesticity'. Thus some middle-class women, denied the opportunity of engaging in the public sphere of paid employment, took it upon themselves to do the 'good work' of visiting the homes of the poor, to educate the women in the ways of 'good housekeeping'. This was largely done through philanthropic societies, which were usually organised and run by men. Jane Lewis (1984, p. 92) points out that this kind of philanthropic work 'involved a fundamental contradiction whereby women left their own homes in order to tell working-class women to stay in theirs'.

If the latter part of the nineteenth century saw the development of leisure provision 'on the rates' by the local state, it was also marked by new forms of commercial leisure provision. Music hall, circus, fairs, horse-racing and the production of literature for a mass market all became highly capitalised (Cunningham, 1980). One area of expansion which was particularly important for leisure was the railway. The availability of rail travel meant a massive increase in family excursions to the seaside or countryside, an important development for women. This trend towards family-oriented activities did in part fit with the middle-class ideology of rational or morally improving pastimes. However,

> The railway gave an enormous boost to unrespectable as well as respectable leisure. There were excursions to public hangings and fairs (Cunningham, 1980, p. 159).

Another feature of this period was the growth in organised sport. Sport grew in popularity and was generally perceived to be a good thing, but was clearly structured along lines of gender and class. The historical development of organised (male) sport has been a favourite topic of leisure historians (Clarke and Critcher, 1985; Cunningham, 1980; Dunning and Sheard, 1979). Women's sport has received substantially less attention. On the whole, opportunities and provision for women lagged far behind those for men. Two partial exceptions were tennis and cycling:

In one major regard tennis was unlike other games: it soon became a game for women as well as men (though female clothing severely restricted their mobility). (Walvin, 1978, p. 93)

Cycling became a focus for a wider political debate:

Cycling was thought to be unladylike (originally of course only ladies tended to ride); it was claimed to be unhealthy, producing various unspecified gynaecological effects, and indecorous, resulting in changes in female clothes. (Walvin, p. 93)

Despite this, women's cycling flourished among upper- and middle-class women, and tennis and croquet were also available to those women who could afford to play. One sport, swimming, was potentially affordable for working-class women in financial terms, through the provision of municipal swimming baths. As Walvin (p. 94) points out, the number of women who were able to make use of these facilities was likely to be low:

It seems unlikely that such pleasures came the way of poorer women whose time and efforts were often totally consumed by family life and whose recreations, as contemporary photographs show, took place on the crowded streets and alleys where they lived.

The changes in leisure that we have illustrated might tempt us into portraying the 1850s onwards as a time of massive expansion in leisure. However, we need to look at what kind of expansion this was. In particular, what were the implications for women? Given that leisure was coming to be firmly understood as free time away from the restrictions of paid work, we are already faced with a problem. For wives and mothers in particular this was simply not the case. Middle-class women were generally excluded from paid work, while working-class women who worked outside the home were also usually responsible for the work of running the home and looking after the family. Indeed, the Victorian ideals of hearth and home promoted this as women's primary role, with paid work coming a poor second. Added to this was the fact that working women were viewed as competitors by their male counterparts, and demarcation between 'men's work' and 'women's work' gained a foothold. This was followed by the downgrading of much women's work, which did nothing to alleviate the existing inequalities in wages.

Social changes were promoting the compartmentalisation of life into discrete areas, but this separation must have meant little to many women. Furthermore, the new kinds of leisure on offer were of limited relevance. They assumed time being available to engage in activities away from the home, and they were organised by the fundamental need to make profit. Working-class women simply did not have this kind of free time, and were unlikely to have money to spare for spending on their own leisure. Whilst middle-class women might have had easier access to spending money, there is no doubt that many of them lived in households characterised by a 'maldistribution' of family resources (Lewis, 1984).

The twentieth century

The twentieth century saw the continuation of the pattern established following industrialisation. Work and leisure were maintained as discrete categories. In terms of leisure provision, the expansion of newer forms in both the commercial and the public sector was matched by the persistence of some elements of traditional working-class culture. So, for example, Roberts (1984) highlights the continuing importance of female friendships and family and social networks. She also comments on how these were often a source of male disapproval.

At the beginning of the twentieth century, the newer forms such as dancing coexisted with walking and church-going as the most popular pastimes. Women's access to each of these varied, and at times was dependent upon a male relative being available to act as chaperon for young, single women. Women had to be careful to appear respectable at all times. Leisure was an area where women's reputations were closely guarded. Dancing in particular was seen as rather risqué, given the opportunities it provided for meeting members of the opposite sex. However, the dances were often organised by churches, so conduct was fairly closely supervised. Many young single women would go to at least two dances each week, and, despite parental efforts, 'managed to find ways of walking home with their young men unsupervised' (Roberts, 1984, p. 71). Although 'beer had few rivals as a form of entertainment either inside or outside the home' (Thompson, 1975), the pub remained a largely male domain. Elizabeth Roberts points this out, commenting that pubs were 'mostly for men or a small number of bolder, older women'. The one area of public and social life where women outnumbered men was religion. The importance of the church, particularly in rural areas, as a legitimate social centre for women should not be underestimated (Thompson, 1975).

The early twentieth century saw the development of an active feminist movement, most visibly the Suffragettes. Although the most obvious outcome of this activity was the granting of the vote to women over the age of thirty-five in 1918, the campaigns were not solely about the vote, but encompassed such things as the need to reform the marriage laws, and early 'wages for housework' campaigns. There was discontent among some middle-class women with the fact that social conventions more or less barred them from paid employment. The status of middle-class men was confirmed by their ability to support wife and family, and the role of the middle-class wife was to devote herself to ensuring that the house was well kept and the needs of other family members attended to. As Cicely Hamilton wrote in 1909, 'Boys are to be happy in themselves, the girls are to make others happy' (quoted in Thompson, 1975, p. 41). Working-class women's campaigns were more likely to concern their own paid employment, and in some cases there were links with trade unionism, despite the prevalent opinion among male workers that women should be excluded.

Paid employment was one area of women's lives that saw significant changes during the 1914-18 war. Women who had never before been employed were encouraged into war work, and women had the opportunity to work in a wide range of jobs:

> One quarter of the 1,600,000 domestic servants took their chance to switch to the new openings for women in munitions and other factories, in

transport and on the land. There was also an influx of women into civil service and commercial occupations. (Thompson, 1975, p. 267)

Not all aspects of doing 'men's work' were positive. Rowbotham notes how protective legislation was set aside, and how women's health suffered through their participation in heavy or dangerous trades. When women were employed in jobs that had been mostly or exclusively male, they were generally paid less than men. But,

> there were significant changes in all women's attitudes to work. The war broke down many of the assumptions which had persisted throughout the industrial revolution. (Rowbotham, 1973, p. 111)

Thompson also comments on the impact of the war on sexual morality – a kind of throwing caution to the wind, with a high illegitimacy rate as one indication of this. However, on the whole, these wartime changes in both employment and sexual behaviour were short-lived. Men returning from the services quickly regained their industrial work. The illegitimacy rate fell, and sexual behaviour returned to the pre-war pattern. Rowbotham argues that the sexual liberation of the post-war period was extremely superficial. There was still a widespread ignorance of contraception, for example, and the 'new freedom' applied only to some young, middle-class women.

During the inter-war years, traditional leisure pursuits faced continuing competition from newer, commercialised forms. This period saw a definite reduction in employment hours, so at least some sectors of society had more time free for leisure. The average worker was employed for just over 50 hours per week in 1910, compared with a typical 60 to 70 hours during the nineteenth century. Many workers had at least a half-day free on Saturdays. Of course, the gender differences in time available for leisure were well entrenched, with the vast majority of women being responsible for domestic labour on top of any paid work.

The newer forms of leisure provision in the commercial sector were geared towards consumption on a mass scale. Perhaps the most significant development in provision was the massive growth of the cinema. The cinema was qualitatively different from other public leisure venues, as it did not share the rather dubious reputation of the music hall. (In fact some music hall owners encouraged a certain number of female customers in order to render their venues more respectable. This was acceptable only in so far as it did not impinge upon the men's enjoyment.) This was an important consideration for women, who could go there without bringing their virtue into question. Another important fact was that the cinema was comparatively cheap, and so it was possible for whole families to attend: 'By the 1920s a new working class habit was developing, that of going together to the cinema on a Saturday night' (Roberts, 1984, p. 123). The cinema had an important function in so far as it could sometimes be used to keep men out of the pub. Gittins (1982) links a decline in pub attendance and drinking with an increase in cinema-going and the development of the cinema as a couple- or family-based leisure institution.

The inter-war years did see a growth of more family-oriented leisure pursuits, alongside an increased emphasis on the home as a site for leisure. This included the wider availability of radios, gramophones and records, books and magazines. In the early days of radio, receivers were prohibitively expensive, but by the 1930s 75 per cent of all families owned a radio. This period was the first in history where the majority of the population were literate, and there was continued expansion in the press, in the use of public libraries, and in the sale of books. The first real growth in publishing for women, at least as far as periodical publishing was concerned, was during the late Victorian years, with forty-eight new titles being launched between 1880 and 1900 (White, 1970). However, during the inter-war years it was not just the amount but also the nature of such publishing that changed. Social and economic changes produced a shift away from the predominantly upper-class 'quality' periodicals toward publications aimed at the middle and lower middle classes. These included many titles which we still see today, such as *Good Housekeeping, Women's Journal, Woman's Own* and *Woman*. The majority of these publications were predominantly concerned with domestic matters, home and family, providing practical suggestions and guide-lines on how to be a successful home-maker, wife and mother. Domestic labour was glorified, and a romantic version of home and family life was promoted. The magazines were a mixture of features, recipes, knitting, sewing, fashion and beauty, short stories and problem-solving. In form, the first mass circulation weeklies, such as *Woman* and *Woman's Own*, have changed little to the present day (Frazer *et al.*, forthcoming).

Documentation of the increased emphasis on family-based leisure tends to under-emphasise the way in which leisure still tended to be strictly gender segregated, and the extent to which it was (and still is) made possible by women's work in the home. There continued to be a significant imbalance between men and women in the amount of time available for leisure. For most women, their limited free time was much more likely to be odd bits of time here and there, rather than being neatly compartmentalised as time free from paid work. However, the move towards smaller families did mean that at least some women were likely to spend less of their time in having and bringing up children.

It is difficult to assess how widespread, in terms of class and region, these changes were; in her study of working-class wives, carried out during the 1930s, Margery Spring Rice found many of her 1,250 research subjects to be living an almost unremitting drudgery, as the following selection of quotations shows:

> Leisure is a comparable term. Anything which is slightly less arduous or gives a change of scene or occupation from the active hard work . . . is leisure.

> . . . out of necessity to rest her legs it seems most leisure will involve having a sit down. Real breaks away from the house are very infrequent and then she often has her children with her.

> An overwhelming proportion say that they spend their leisure in sewing and doing other household jobs, slightly different from the ordinary work of cooking and house-cleaning. (Spring Rice, 1939, p. 99)

In terms of leisure activities, the cinema was hardly mentioned, and 'many women said they had never been to the pictures' because it proved too expensive. 'The wireless' was also beyond the means of the poorer homes. Some of the rural women mentioned walking, gardening or going to church or chapel as their leisure interests. Women with children were usually only able to have some rest once the children were in bed, by which time they themselves would have been on their feet for twelve to fourteen hours.

Leaving the house during the day would either be for essential errands, shopping and so on, or might involve a visit to the infant welfare clinic. Spring Rice attributes the success of these clinics at least in part to the fact that women greatly enjoyed an afternoon away from the home in the company of 'kindly doctors and nurses as well as other women with whom she can talk'. This is a prime example of women creating their own leisure in the face of adverse conditions and an illustration of the way in which women often gain some vicarious pleasure for themselves through their roles as mothers. Another way in which women were able to carve out a little time and space for themselves was by going to visit friends and neighbours who were often in a similar position. Again, the importance of female support networks is clear. Other trips outside the home were few and far between, particularly in the evenings when a woman could not leave the children, 'unless her husband undertakes to keep house for one evening a week whilst she goes to the pictures or for a walk' (Spring Rice, 1939). Even this small degree of co-operation was not always forthcoming, and women's difficulties could be compounded by the fact that many of them did not have any clothes considered suitable for a day or evening out.

What Spring Rice's study highlights is the way in which access to the expanding 'leisure market' was differentiated. Spring Rice had very clear ideas about what steps should be taken to improve the lot of working-class women. She suggested the provision of well-equipped commercial wash-houses and bake-houses which would relieve some of the drudgery and allow women to meet other women. She also advocated local women's clubs, near to home, where women could go 'to seek rest and companionship, cultural and recreative occupation and blessed change of scene'. Finally, she advocated that housewives should have at least one week's holiday with pay per year. Modest though these demands were, few have been met, apart from during the exceptional circumstances of wartime.

The expansion within the leisure sector generally and the growth of highly capitalised forms available to a mass audience specifically could be interpreted as an example of the 'growth' of leisure. What we need to understand is the precise nature of the 'leisure' that was expanding. By the mid twentieth century, the commercial sector was by and large established as the place where leisure needs were met. Other forms of provision, notably through the local state, seem to have still been predominantly of the baths, parks and gardens variety. We should also take note of the voluntary sector as an important area for leisure activity; although this too was structured along lines of gender, race and class, women do have a history of involvement in voluntary organisations, clubs and societies. However, for the majority of people, leisure was increasingly commercialised. Provision was obviously profit-oriented, and there was a growing emphasis on advertising as a means of reaching consumers. One crucial consideration that is often missing from conventional accounts is the different ways in which men and women have been historically constructed as consumers. Whilst men were being addressed in their own right as consumers of leisure, women were primarily addressed as consumers within the domestic sphere. Women's spending power was based around their roles as home-makers. The exceptions to this were young, single, employed women, and as Sheila Rowbotham (1973, p. 125) points out, 'In fact change in the leisure industry meant that cosmetics, cheaper clothes and the film industry expanded along with the earning power of young women white-collar workers'. Gender was not the only division in access to the leisure market: 'Region, class and gender were factors which differentiated access to the market and its partial scope' (Clarke and Critcher, 1985, p. 75).

We have already noted how the First World War brought about a disruption to conventional morality, at least for some sections of the population. To some extent the same must have been true of the Second World War. There is also no doubt that once again one of the most important implications for women was their participation in the labour force. Many more women became accustomed to earning their own income and to having some of the associated freedoms, albeit within a climate of wartime austerity. For the first time many of them were solely responsible for their families. This posed obvious problems once the war was over and the men returned, as a letter to a contemporary magazine at the time illustrates:

> I am one of the many women whose husbands have returned from the forces and who suddenly find themselves without the crowding activities forced upon them during the war . . . Now that I am solely a housewife again, I am finding life very quiet. (*Everywoman*, 1946, quoted in White, 1970, p. 133)

'The Lady' also comments on the problem of how women are to gain acceptance in civilian life for newer modes of behaviour in the area of leisure:

> The attitudes of women of all classes to the 'local' has had to be adjusted in the war years. Girls in the services, away from home, have learned to use the public houses and to go to them with men friends in a decorous way, and it is unlikely that when these girls marry or get into civilian employment again they will be willing to forgo these cheerful meetings.

The popular magazines offered a range of advice on personal and emotional problems. However, in relation to women's employment, the majority of the publications went down the traditional line and discouraged women from continuing to work outside the home. With the men home again, women were under considerable pressure to return to the pre-war pattern, although of course many women continued to go out to work from economic necessity. A few magazines, certainly the minority, did put forward the opinion that women should be able to combine a home and family with a career if they so wished. It is worth noting that many of the debates around (married) women's right to employment were couched in terms of employment being an 'outside interest' rather than a career.

Though wartime austerity continued through the 1940s and early 1950s, during the war leisure had been seen as an important element in keeping spirits high, and in the post-war period, 'it was perhaps because of continuing hardships that enjoyment became a national obsession in the late 1940s . . . the immediate post-war years were a boom period for British leisure industries' (Walvin, 1978, p. 149). Whilst this is undoubtedly true, there is also no doubt that significant sections of society, including many women, were not fully able to take advantage of the boom. One activity which did retain its popularity with (predominantly working-class) women was cinema attendance, with 1946 being a record year. The 1940s also saw the highest ever public attendance at football matches. After the 1938 Holidays With Pay Act, more and more people were going away on holidays, particularly to seaside resorts and mainly as families. However, this was still beyond the reach of many: in 1949 three-quarters of families with three or more children took their holidays at home (Walvin, 1978).

From the 1950s onwards Britain entered a period of considerable social and economic change. A higher proportion of women in the labour force meant a rise in family incomes. The labour market had changed in other ways too: 'Unemployment effectively disappeared during the war and remained scarcely significant during the 1950s, a decade when consumer spending almost doubled' (Walvin, 1978, p. 152). There was increased spending on 'non-essential' consumer durables manufactured in the new light industries and promoted by advertising. Women as consumers continued to be addressed as keepers of the family purse. A point worth emphasising is the extent to which household artefacts were marketed as leisure goods for women. Presenting women's work as leisure was perhaps epitomised by one manufacturer naming a particular model of gas cooker the 'Leisure' cooker, with each one bearing this rather dubious title. This is just one particularly unsubtle way of telling us that our domestic labour is not real work, but is in fact leisure.

Social historians who deal with the post-war period are careful to point out that much of the growth in consumption was due to a massive rise in consumer credit, a rise which has continued its upward trend to the present day. Walvin lists the most important material acquisitions as cars, motorcycles, televisions, irons, fridges and washing machines. No doubt these did positively change family life, and perhaps the improved and more widely available domestic appliances did lighten women's workload. In terms of leisure, cars and televisions were important for family leisure, although this is not to say that all family members have equal access to them. The continuing shift was clearly toward privatised domestic consumption as leisure. Public attendance at cinemas and sporting events declined. In fact sport itself changed substantially with the advent of televised sport, and the increasing importance of advertising and sponsorship. As far as women are concerned, what is perhaps important is the supreme indifference of many women to much televised sport. This is not entirely surprising, given the kinds of sport that predominate and indeed the nature of the coverage itself. The historical divisions within sport and the marginalisation of women's participation in sport are reproduced through the broadcast media.

Certainly, the decline in cinema-going had greater implications for women than did the fall in football spectatorship. Despite the shift towards home-based leisure, there was still a market for an activity that appealed mainly to working-class women. Bingo became extremely popular, being one of the few (fairly) socially acceptable ways for women to spend their leisure time outside the home. Like other forms of gambling it also offered the potential for winning. Neither the periodic moral panics over women supposedly gambling away the housekeeping nor the dismissal of the game itself as 'mindless' by the uninitiated served to diminish its popularity.

One crucial feature of the post-war British expansion was the encouragement and subsequent direct recruitment of workers from the West Indies. As Fryer (1984) points out, black people have been

living in Britain for almost five hundred years. T
immigrants arrived in Britain in the late 1940s, a
following ten years some 125,000 West Indians settled
there were also around 55,000 immigrants from the
continent. The majority of these immigrant workers had t
low-paid, low-status jobs – jobs which, as Fryer points out   . +),
'the local white population did not want'. They and their families
faced direct discrimination in terms of housing and employment.
They also encountered racist attitudes from the majority of the white
British population, and physical and/or verbal abuse from some.

Clarke and Critcher (1985) state that the 'shameful history of
immigration to Britain' has had an influence on leisure during the
last thirty or so years. They suggest that this influence has taken two
forms: first, the development of cultural ghettoes whereby members
of ethnic minorities necessarily preserved and developed their own
culture apart from mainstream racist white culture; and second, the
development of ethnic entrepreneurship within the leisure market,
mostly centred around food.

Conclusion

Attempting to uncover the history of women's leisure is an uphill
struggle, given the paucity of material that is available. The process
of industrialisation brought great changes to the lives of the
majority of the British population, and provided the framework
within which we still understand and define leisure. The separation
of work and leisure into discrete categories meant that women's
leisure as well as men's came to be defined in terms of their
relationship to paid work. The sexual division of labour and the
location of women firmly within the domestic sphere (regardless of
their actual employment status) rendered leisure a problematic
concept for women. In practice, women's responsibility for home
and family has meant that most women have never had the same
kind of unambiguously free time as men: nor have they generally
had access to the same degree of spending power. Of course, there
are obvious class differences in both these respects. However, an
examination of the histories of working-class and middle-class
women point to two indisputable facts: first, women's opportunities

for leisure have been much more restricted than men's; and second, women's leisure needs have rarely been understood or met.

The next three chapters indicate how little change there has been in the prime causes of gender inequality in access to leisure. Although social change may have modified the precise content of negotiations about women's leisure opportunities, nevertheless relationships with male partners, an unequal division of childcare and domestic labour, the demands of paid work, and prevailing norms about appropriate behaviour still circumscribe women's freedoms. The singers may have changed and the lyrics are slightly different, but the song remains substantially the same as a century or more ago.

4

Women's leisure today

Gender differences in leisure patterns

What little we know about women's leisure indicates that the activities women enjoy and do most frequently in and around the home are not much different from men's preferred forms of leisure. The 1983 *General Household Survey*, a British government publication based on interviews with a representative national sample of over 10,000 women and nearly 9,000 men aged over 16, showed that 98 per cent of both the women and the men had watched television in the month period to the interview; 86 per cent of the women and 87 per cent of the men had listened to the radio; and nearly two-thirds of the respondents – 62 per cent of the women and 65 per cent of the men – had played records or tapes at home (see Table 4.10). Gender differences were more marked for reading, gardening, do-it-yourself, sewing and knitting: more women do reading and crafts, while more men do DIY and gardening. Another national survey of 2,000 people aged 15 and over, also carried out in 1983, likewise found that watching television and listening to the radio and music were the three most popular leisure activities, and were done by equal numbers of men and women (NOP, 1983). Again, reading books, knitting and sewing were more popular with women, and gardening and do-it-yourself were for men, with at least 20 per cent more of one gender than the other doing each of these activities.

Table 4.1   *Social activities and hobbies:*
participation by males and females aged 16 and over

Percentages participating in the following activities in the four weeks
before interview.

	Males	*Females*
Social activities and hobbies		
- not on prompt list[1]		
Bingo	5	11
Betting ⎫	5 ⎫ 28	1 ⎫ 12
Football pools ⎭	25 ⎭	11 ⎭
Other gambling	1	1
Playing games of skill	16	12
Dancing	10	12
Clubs/Societies	11	12
Voluntary work	7	9
Hobbies/crafts/arts	11	3
Cooking/wine/preserve making	1	1
Animal keeping	2	1
Leisure classes (excl. sports, dancing)	1	2
Amateur music/drama (excl. classes)	3	3
Total doing at least one activity[2]	60	52
excl. leisure classes and amateur music/drama		
- on prompt list[3]		
Visiting/entertaining friends/relations	90	93
Going out for a meal ⎫	41 ⎫ 73	40 ⎫ 60
Going out for a drink ⎭	64 ⎭	46 ⎭
Watching TV	98	98
Listening to radio	87	86
Listening to records/tapes	65	62
Reading books	50	61
Gardening	50	39
DIY	51	24
Dressmaking/needlework/knitting	2	48
Total doing at least one activity	100	100
	N = 8,744	N = 10,306

Notes to Table 4.1

[1] These activities were not included on the prompt list and were therefore not asked about specifically. All of them except cooking/wine/preserve making and animal keeping were however included on the aide-memoire card.

[2] Total includes those activities not separately listed (see Table 10.22 of the *General Household Survey* 1983).

[3] These activities were on the prompt list and were therefore asked about specifically.

Source: adapted from the *General Household Survey* 1983 and reproduced by kind permission of the Controller of Her Majesty's Stationery Office.

If we examine patterns of leisure participation away from home, the picture changes to one of much greater gender differentiation. More men than women do out-of-home activities in general, and both the GHS and NOP surveys report men to be much more likely to go out drinking, to gamble and to engage in sporting activities, both indoors and outdoors. Youth and social class position cut across gender differences to promote participation in leisure activities away from home.

Women's lower participation rates than men in sporting activities have been recognised for some time. The *General Household Survey* 1983 shows that almost 20 per cent more men than women had taken part in sports, games and physical activities in the month prior to interview, and their patterns of participation in various sports are very different (see Table 4.2). Whereas walking is the most popular single activity for both men and women, yoga or keep fit and swimming were the only other activities done by more than one woman in twenty. For men, in contrast, football, snooker/billiards/ pool, darts and swimming all came into this category, with various other activities almost attaining this level of popularity, such as golf, fishing and squash. (Patterns of women's participation in sport will be discussed in more detail later in this chapter).

Table 4.2   *Participation in sports, games and physical activities by males and females aged 16 and over*

Percentages participating in the following activities in the four weeks before interview.

	Males	Females
Outdoor		
Walking 2 miles or more	20	18
Football	6	-
Golf	4	1
Fishing	4	-
Swimming	4	4
Athletics	3	1
Cycling	2	2
Bowls	2	-
Tennis	1	1
Total doing at least one activity	39	24
Indoor		
Snooker/billiards/pool	15	2
Darts	11	4
Swimming	7	7
Keep fit/Yoga	-	5
Squash	4	1
Badminton	2	2
Table Tennis	2	2
Bowls/tenpin bowling	1	1
Total doing at least one activity	33	18
	N = 8,744	10,306

Source: adapted from the General Household Survey 1983, Tables 10.5 and 10.6, and reproduced by kind permission of the Controller of Her Majesty's Stationery Office.

The 'big five' most popular leisure activities are, it is asserted, drinking, gambling, watching television, sex and playing football. It does not take a very profound analysis to work out that very few women play football (less than 1 per cent, according to the GHS). Whilst most women, like most men, may watch television, drink alcohol, have sex and gamble, how they do it and what it means to them are likely to be different and hence to provide qualitatively different kinds of leisure experience. Gambling for men mainly takes the form of football pools and horse-race betting: 28 per cent of all men bet in this way, and 5 per cent play bingo. In contrast, only 12 per cent of women engage in these forms of betting, and 11 per cent play bingo. The GHS data and the Dixey and Talbot study (1982) reveal the socio-demographic profile of the typical bingo player to be elderly and of working class. The divergent experiences of women and men in relation to alcohol, sexuality and watching television are discussed at various points in this book, so it is necessary here only to point out that simplistic comparisons of gender differences in leisure are unlikely to contribute significantly to our understanding of the reasons underlying those differences.

The findings of the major British surveys are borne out by smaller localised studies of the impact of gender on leisure. These include Deem's (1986a) study of women's leisure in the new town of Milton Keynes; Dixey and Talbot's (1982) study of women residents of Armley, an established working-class district in the northern industrial city of Leeds; Wimbush's (1986) study of Edinburgh mothers with young children; and our own study of Sheffield women (Green, Hebron and Woodward, 1987b). All of these studies confirm the national survey data on the popularity of watching television, reading, and doing home-based crafts for women. Using sources such as these, which provide qualitative data about the place of leisure in women's lives as a whole, it is possible to offer explanations for the patterns of leisure activity noted in these and the large surveys. We cannot only construct a picture of women's leisure activities within and outside the home, but can also indicate how far leisure patterns are a reflection of women's social situation – their age group, their social class, their own and their male partner's employment status, their domestic situation and ethnic identity, as well as their geographical location.

Despite the regional diversity of these studies, a series of common themes clearly emerge concerning the way in which such variations in women's personal circumstances are experienced in relation to leisure. We can begin to identify the social processes that shape the leisure experiences of young women as they grow up, and to show how marriage and motherhood and their position in the labour market structure women's recreational opportunities, by drawing on other studies of the lives led by these groups of women to supplement our limited knowledge of their leisure activities. As yet we have much less qualitative information available about the lives and leisure of older women – which may well reflect the low level of visibility and status of the elderly and their concerns in our society – and of women from ethnic minority groups. These are major gaps in our understanding, and this research urgently needs to be done to inform theory and policy.

Researching women's leisure

Many of the empirical studies of women's lives and leisure on which this chapter and the next, on work and leisure, are based, share a feminist approach to their subject matter. This involves more than just determining what women's patterns of recreation are, and seeking to explain them in terms of the prevailing paradigms in social science. It requires that they should be understood as part and parcel of the women's lives as a whole, and seen through the eyes of the women respondents themselves. This perspective belongs to the tradition of Weber's *Verstehensociologie* in the sense of aiming to understand the meanings and motivations which those being studied attach to their behaviour. It shares the same goal of seeking insight through empathy, even though it derives from different origins, namely the politics of the Women's Movement. Thus the activities (or inactivities!) that women spend time doing need to be analysed within the framework of their lives as a whole. What time do women have available for leisure, after the obligations of paid work and unpaid domestic labour have been met? And what material, cultural and ideological constraints restrict women's access to leisure time and their choices about how it may be spent? How do these constraints operate: are they the result of self-imposed 'policing' attributable to women's desire to earn the community's respect and to avoid its censure, or are they the result of norms being enforced on their behaviour by others? Without this broad contextual setting, research does not take us much beyond the *General Household Survey's* tables of the percentages of men and women doing various activities. In order to go further than merely documenting and counting women's participation in leisure activities we need to have the theoretical and empirical evidence available to help us explain not just how gender influences leisure, but how gender is constructed, interpreted, perceived and experienced, for all the social groups that comprise this half of the population.

There is now an established body of literature in the social sciences on gender inequalities and differences in relation to various major social institutions, such as the family, employment, education, health, welfare, the media and the law. We are witnessing the beginnings of such a literature in the field of leisure studies. Many constraints on leisure opportunities clearly apply both to men and women, such as the restrictions of paid employment and parenting on leisure time, or the constraining effects of poverty and loneliness. However, there is evidence to show that these factors impinge in different ways, and to a greater or lesser extent on women than on men as a reflection of contemporary definitions of gender roles. Some constraints apply to most women, but to few men, such as the fear of being out alone after dark. The Second British Crime Survey (Hough and Mayhew, 1985) found that half the women interviewed only went out after dark if accompanied, and 40 per cent were 'very worried' about being raped. Over half of the respondents in the Sheffield gender and leisure survey were worried about being out alone after dark and most of these women saw it as a 'big problem' for them (Green, Hebron and Woodward, 1987b). Although one might expect that women from affluent households who have access to a private car would be less affected by this anxiety than other women, in fact the similar proportion of women from a diverse range of social backgrounds who share this worry is striking. The Greater London Council's Women's Committee study of women and transport also found high levels of anxiety about using Underground and bus services and walking at night-time (GLC, 1985). Thirty per cent of respondents strongly agreed with the statement 'I don't go out on my own after dark', a proportion rising from about a sixth of the young women to well over half of the over-sixties. Women who know of other women who have been attacked or harassed become more alert to what is going on around them, and may become less willing to go out after dark. The report says: 'It is clear that a very high proportion of elderly and Asian women in particular are severely restricted in their activities at night by fear of attack, and have adjusted their lives to avoid the need to go out alone' (p. 8).

Evidently, then, many women circumscribe their leisure activities outside the home because of worries about their safety, and this constraint affects women's mobility much more than men's. Other constraints apply to both women and men in particular social groups, for example those in the same age group or social class group, but we would argue that even here gender is often a significant source of difference. Elderly men on low incomes who are lonely still have the choice open to them of going to the pub or working men's club, even if one drink may have to last them half the evening, whereas this is not seen as a viable leisure activity for a similarly placed woman. Ninety-three per cent of the Sheffield survey respondents said they would feel uncomfortable going into a working men's club on their own (and in many parts of northern Britain these clubs are the focal point for recreation and sociability in the community), and 84 per cent felt the same way about going into a pub. Women's feelings of being unwelcome in public houses if unaccompanied by men have also been reported from studies done elsewhere in Britain and other Anglo-Saxon cultures (Whitehead, 1976; Dempsey, 1987; Woodward and Green, in Wimbush and Talbot, 1988).

Class position, income level, work situation, age, domestic circumstances and stage in the family life-cycle, as well ethnicity, all have a major bearing on how women experience leisure, making global generalisations about women's leisure unsafe and probably inaccurate for many women. Some of these variables have a direct impact on access to leisure, and others are mediated through commonsense assumptions about appropriate and respectable behaviour, and how men may treat women. These are major issues running through many of the chapters in this book. For example, being a member of a low-income household may of itself limit spending on leisure activities, but even within such household units its members are not seen as equally entitled to personal spending money for leisure outside the home. This point comes out clearly from studies of, for example, the spending patterns of the households of unemployed men, as we shall see in Chapter 5. We therefore need to consider how gender influences women's experiences of leisure, not just in terms of the issues that affect most if not all women, such as feeling vulnerable outside the home after dark, but also to examine how gender issues operate differently for women from the various social groups.

This chapter attempts to establish how gender is experienced by women from a diverse range of social backgrounds and personal circumstances in influencing their access to free time and its use. To do this we can draw on the kinds of data sets already mentioned – large national surveys and local studies of women's leisure – but the paucity of such material means that it will not take us very far in exploring the impact of gender across the range of social divisions. We therefore need to supplement this material with a re-reading of a much wider range of studies on women in households of varying sizes and levels of affluence, in different ethnic groups and through the life course, to elicit information about women's leisure experiences. Although few of these studies include 'leisure' as an item in the index, in fact a close reading of them offers the reader a wealth of empirical material about gender differences in access to free time, in norms about entitlement to leisure, and about the context of cultural beliefs within which negotiations about leisure take place. Even if information of this kind is not explicitly presented in these studies, it is useful to explore what they can tell us about the nature of women's daily lives. More specifically, information about women's status as housewives, unpaid carers, or as paid workers, as partners in relationships or as women living alone, helps us discern how associated constraints promote or circumscribe their access to and use of free time.

These are important issues to keep in mind as a contextual framework for exploring gender inequalities in access to leisure. The next section of the chapter focuses on women's involvement in physical recreation, drawing particularly on the findings of the Sheffield study. Taking sport as an important example of an area of leisure activity, we can see the cumulative impact of certain variables and how they operate in advantaging or disadvantaging women's participation rates. The final part of the chapter contains a series of case studies which describe the lifestyles, circumstances and structural situation of selected contrasting groups of women. Using material drawn from a variety of sources, the aim is to identify the leisure experiences of women from a range of socio-demographic categories and across social divisions, highlighting which aspects of their situation promote or facilitate, and which constrain or restrict their opportunities to enjoy autonomous leisure.

Women's participation in physical recreation

Earlier in this chapter we saw that, according to large-scale data sets such as the *General Household Survey*, men and women tend to engage in broadly similar leisure activities in and around the home, but their recreation patterns diverge considerably away from home. This applies particularly to physical recreation, which is done by 54 per cent of men compared with 35 per cent of women (*General Household Survey* 1983). In the Sheffield study, 35.2 per cent of the 707 survey respondents said that they did some kind of sport, which is remarkably close to the GHS figure of 35 per cent, especially given our less rigorous criterion of participation. Deem's (1986a) study of a random sample of Milton Keynes women also yielded about one-third of respondents who regularly did sport of some kind. As in her study, the Sheffield survey found that for women, yoga and keep fit were by far the most popular physical recreation activities, followed by swimming, badminton, tennis, squash, and running or jogging (see Table 4.3).

Whilst the Sheffield survey data provide information about the socio-demographic profile of participants in these various activities, the numbers of respondents on which this information is based are too small to permit reliable inferences to be drawn. We are on rather safer ground when we look at the characteristics of the group of women participants in sport as a whole, women doing yoga or keep fit, and women who watch live sport. The tendency to do these activities is significantly associated with a large number of factors, including age, stage in the life-cycle, employment status, terminal education age, social class, personal and household income level, and both respondents' and partners' employment status. These relationships suggest that advantageous personal circumstances promote participation in physical recreation; youth, being in employment, having achieved a high level of education, being middle class and having a high income are correlated with high participation rates.

Table 4.3 *Sheffield gender and leisure survey: women's participation in physical recreation*

1. Percentages of respondents doing specified activities at the time of interview:

Yoga/keep fit	(N = 170)	24
Watching live sport	(N = 100)	15
Swimming	(N = 66)	10
Badminton	(N = 57)	8
Tennis	(N = 42)	6
Squash	(N = 28)	4
Running/jogging	(N = 28)	4
Other	(N = 33)	5
No. doing at least one activity	(N = 236)	35

Survey total = 707

2. Frequency of participation in specified activities (currently or in season, per cent):

		Daily/several times a week	Weekly	Once or twice a week	Less often
Playing sport	(N = 166)	32	41	15	8
Doing keep fit/yoga	(N = 170)	33	50	13	7
Watching live sport	(N = 100)	12	43	33	21

Survey total = 707

Note
For detailed results of the survey in tabular form, see Appendix 3 in Green, Hebron and Woodward, 1987b. Appendix 4 provides data on statistically significant correlations for some of the activities discussed here, and further discussion is included in Woodward, Green and Hebron, 1989.

As one might expect, women aged under 35 play more sport, including yoga and keep fit, than older women, and single women do so more than married women, with or without children. One-third of women aged between 18 and 34 do yoga or keep fit, a proportion which falls off markedly with increasing age. Participation in sport in general falls steadily from one in three of the youngest age group down to one in eight of the 45 to 59 year-old women. Watching sport, although less popular than actually taking part in it, is also done more by the younger women. Family situation is an important determinant of women's involvement in physical recreation. The single women's high participation rates appear to fall by half on marriage, and are lowest of all for the group of lone parents. Otherwise, however, the patterns of participation are not regular, unilinear ones.

The popularity of doing physical recreation, although declining consistently with increasing age, is less predictable in relation to the effect of other variables. The mothers of under-fives, for example, may find it difficult to watch live sport, but one in four of them still manage to do some physical recreation activity. Marriage seems, for these respondents, to have a more depressing effect on participation than does the arrival of children. This may indicate that mothers do manage to make opportunities for doing sport more often then childless wives do; or it may be that much of a mother's physical recreation is not so much independent leisure as family leisure. Given the popularity of swimming, for example, it could be that what we are counting as instances of women's participation in sport may in practice be mothers' opportunities to spend an hour bent double in lukewarm water helping their children to swim! Part of the popularity of swimming may come from its scope for family leisure: few other sports permit simultaneous participation from those of different age groups and levels of proficiency. However, this raises the question of whether time spent accompanying children swimming constitutes personal leisure and an opportunity for physical recreation, or whether it is merely an extension of women's role as mothers.

The tendency to play sport increases with both social class and terminal education age. For yoga and keep fit this is particularly marked, with 30 per cent of the women in the upper and middle social class groups doing it compared with only 14 per cent of women from the lower working-class groups (based on partner's occupation). Likewise, women from households with the highest annual incomes were twice as likely as women from the lowest income group to engage in physical recreation; and those with the highest terminal education age were three times more likely to play sport and do yoga or keep fit than those who left school at 14 to 15 years old. Working-class women (whether classified on the basis of their own or their partner's occupation) were only about half as likely to do or to watch sport as middle-class women. Despite the inroads into their time made by full-time employment, working women had higher rates of both participation in and watching live sport than did women in part-time employment and those currently not working outside the home. The partners of employed men were much more likely to do or to watch sport than were the wives of unemployed men; only in relation to keep fit and yoga did these women's participation rates come anywhere near those for the wives of employed men, and even then only half as many did them. The wives of employed men were six times as likely to play other sports and three times as likely to watch live sport as the wives of unemployed men.

As far as participation in specific sports activities in concerned, the patterns that emerge for these Sheffield women do bear out other data on the popularity of various activities. Keep fit and yoga were the most popular sports for women at all stages of the life-cycles, followed by swimming. Badminton was the next most popular activity for all groups except the mothers of small children. Tennis was popular with the single women and the married women with no children – groups which included most of the younger women respondents – but squash and running or jogging tended to be less popular activities for women in each group.

Taken together, these data support the observations already made about the accumulation of advantages or disadvantages for women's leisure associated with age, family situation and material or financial resources.

Social identity and leisure

This chapter has so far examined material from national and local studies about women's leisure patterns, and has sought to identify those variables which influence women's access to time free for leisure, and the range of activities available to them. Some of these influences are clear-cut and fairly self-evident, for example age and family situation: young, single women typically have more leisure time and personal spending money than their older, married sisters with small children. In order to understand women's leisure adequately, however, we must look beyond these superficial comparisons to identify the web of cultural norms and practices within which people live out their lives, such as those associated with being a 'good' daughter, wife or mother, and to establish the social processes which generate and perpetuate these moral codes. The ideologies within which these social roles are generated and maintained influence patterns of the domestic division of labour, women's position in the labour market and financial arrangements within the home; they also influence women's own expectations and aspirations, and those of their intimate associates.

These issues are addressed in depth in other chapters. Here we identify pertinent aspects of them in order to inform our discussion and to set the context for a detailed analysis of the lives and leisure of two under-researched and relatively powerless groups of women within society, namely black women and elderly women. The Women's Movement in Britain has recently been making strenuous efforts to redress its implicitly 'white' focus (Ramazanoglu, 1989), but as yet we lack sufficient information from autobiographies, fiction, empirical studies and other sources to provide more than partial and incomplete accounts of the lives and experiences of black women. Elderly women are similarly almost invisible in terms of research, politics and public policy: they remain a large but isolated minority within the population. The leisure needs of both groups of women merit much more attention than they have hitherto received.

There are, of course, other neglected groups of women within society whose interests and needs are virtually ignored by researchers, leisure providers, the media and the general public. Disabled women and lesbians are yet to be identified as recreationally disadvantaged in terms of existing provision in most parts of the country, and information on their specific needs and leisure patterns is very sparse.

Black women's lives and leisure in Britain

Black women in Britain share a gender identity and skin colour, and experience discrimination on both counts, but cultural and social structural differences make it meaningless to attempt to describe their lives in terms of one simple stereotype. This label encompasses groups of women as diverse as those who have recently arrived in

Britain, to marry or to join relatives, from rural peasant communities in India, Pakistan and Bangladesh, as well as women from the same ethnic group who belonged to prosperous petit-bourgeois families in East Africa prior to their expulsion a decade and a half ago. It includes Afro-Caribbean women from different West Indian islands, each with a distinctive cultural heritage, who have lived and worked in Britain for a generation, and also their daughters who may have been born here and grown up within British society; and it includes groups of black women from western, eastern and southern African countries who have come here, alone or with husbands, to study or to work. The two largest groups of black women in Britain today are those of Afro-Caribbean origin and South Asian women, and what little literature exists on the lives of black women in Britain mainly deals with these two groups.

The Afro-Caribbean community of West Indian origin in Britain is about half a million strong, including the children of West Indian parents who were born here. About half of these originated in Jamaica, with others coming from Trinidad, Guyana, Barbados, St. Kitts and elsewhere in the Caribbean (Driver, 1982). Centuries of exploitative colonial trading between Britain and the West Indies in agricultural commodities, manufactured goods and slaves, have meant that West Indians and Africans have been a feature of British society, albeit in small numbers, for two hundred years. Those cities with the strongest mercantile links with the New World, notably Bristol, Liverpool and Cardiff, have had established communities of black residents in inner-city areas and near the docks since long before the major wave of West Indian immigration of the 1950s and 1960s. This later influx was part of a major post-war migration to North America and Britain that was stimulated by the collapse in the prices for plantation crops during the depression of the 1920s and 1930s, from which West Indian agriculture failed to recover. After the war Britain needed a cheap supply of labour for reconstruction and industrial expansion. Its ostensible cultural affinity as 'Mother Country' for many of the Caribbean islands made it a potent economic magnet for those who could see little prospect of escape from grinding poverty and acute unemployment at home (Bryan, Dadzie and Scafe, 1985).

This migration was unusual in that almost as many young single women as young men, came; also, some older men and women came, leaving their children in the care of female relatives. A more common pattern is for the first wave of migrants to consist predominantly of young single men, who initially see themselves as temporary residents, and may in the course of time 'bring out' marriageable women from their own country. Although this pattern may be disrupted by legal restrictions on migration or by the requirements or practices of employing organisations, as in the cases of recent New Commonwealth immigration to Britain and white colonial emigration from Britain to India and Africa in the nineteenth century, the common corollary of primary migration is a distortion in the age structure of the immigrant population which may endure for a couple of generations. Until the migrant group includes grandparents and small children as well as adults of working age, the family structures of the home society are distorted. New patterns of familial relationships develop as traditional practices are modified in the context of the changed conditions of employment and housing in the host society, with consequent effects on patterns of social interaction and sociability.

In the case of the Afro-Caribbean community in Britain, several studies have traced the adaptation of indigenous household patterns that had evolved in response to conditions of servitude, poverty and colonial agricultural practices in the West Indies, to help individuals to cope with the changed conditions of life and work in Britain (Patterson, 1965; Barrow, 1982; Driver, 1982). Barrow describes this 'readaptation' of the family types that had become established patterns in the West Indies, to fit better the exigencies of life in the 'Mother Country'. The most common household forms found in the West Indies after the Second World War were:

1. The conventional nuclear family household, also known in this context as 'Christian marriage'. It has mainly been found among the economically better off (based on property owner-ship, professional status, or steady employment) and/or the more religious members of the community.

2. The common-law family household, where couples live together who are not formally married, and they care for the children of the household, who may or may not be theirs biologically. (The couple may legitimise their union with a marriage ceremony in middle age).

3. The matrifocal household, where the mother or grandmother of the children is the sole stable head of the household.

The second and third household types are characteristically associated with conditions of material privation, and can be seen as one of the legacies of slavery and colonialism. The ideal of the Victorian family with an authoritative male head of the household is one that few households can attain, in the context of very high rates of male unemployment. Heavy male emigration during and after the Second World War represented no radical departure from the tradition of matrifocal rural households, whose menfolk may be absent for long periods in search of work; in any case they were largely irrelevant to the family's economic subsistence. Men's negligible financial role in helping to support such households, and their consequent lack of power and authority within it, can be traced back to the social conditions associated with slavery, when stable unions between slaves were neither recognised nor respected by slave-owners. The basic household unit was therefore the mother and her children. Various features of the West Indian experience in Britain served to maintain women's high level of responsibility for the economic sustenance of the household, as well as its support in domestic and emotional terms, although the social costs of this pattern are high for women isolated from the support of relatives and friends.

The main form of employment available to both male and female West Indian immigrants have been, and continue to be, in the worst paid, lowest status, most insecure and uncongenial parts of the labour market. Thirty years of racism from both employers and fellow-workers has created a *de facto* segregation of employment opportunities, and currently contributes to much higher levels of black than white unemployment. The economic pressures on West Indian men and women coming to Britain in search of a higher standard of living and better educational opportunities for their children were a powerful motivation for both women and men to maximise their earnings (Patterson, 1965). In the context of manual employment, this has meant working overtime, shiftwork, and unsocial hours. The experience of long hours of hard, physical work in order to make a living, in addition to running a home and rearing children, was by no means a new experience for women from the West Indies – such had been their lot under slavery and in colonial agriculture – but the absence of their traditional support network of female relatives was new. Barrow (1982) describes the system of shared, communal childrearing found in most Caribbean societies.

Despite their poverty, their children enjoyed close relationships with a range of adult carers who had the time and motivation to play with them, tell them stories, and keep an eye on them while they enjoyed creative and stimulating activities with whatever materials were available in and around the home. Material poverty was off-set by the warmth of extended family relationships and the tropical climate. In the context of poor housing in the cold climate of Britain's inner cities, Afro-Caribbean women in Britain have been forced by a shortage of adequate state facilities for the care of pre-school children into using private childminding arrangements, as a substitute for the Caribbean system of childcare. The economic and social pressures on the childminders make it difficult for them to provide the same quality of care that children in the West Indies receive, and Barrow attributes part of the underachievement of West Indian children in the British education system to this early disadvantage. This is compounded in adolescence by the young people's experience of racism and the dearth of black role models in positions of authority and achievement.

Leisure opportunities for the older generation of West Indian women have been subject to major constraints in this social, cultural and economic context. Long hours of physically hard, alienating work and unsocial working hours, coupled with the responsibility of maintaining a home and family, leave little time for women factory workers of whatever skin colour to enjoy leisure (see, for example, Cavendish, 1982). The financial barriers to having leisure away from home, which usually entails spending money on doing an activity, travel, equipment or refreshments, are compounded by cultural and social barriers (Patterson, 1965). Isolation from an extended network of female kin removes a source both of childcare and of leisure companions. The fear of racist harassment on the streets and of discrimination in leisure venues have been further potent discouragements to venturing outside the home for recreation. Quantitative evidence to support these assertions comes from the recent study on women and transport conducted by the Greater London Council (GLC, 1984). The pressures on Afro-Caribbean women's time and finances associated with higher levels of employment than other groups of women, their lower incomes and lower levels of access to private cars, showed themselves in significantly lower frequencies of travel to and from leisure activities. Only a third of the Afro-Caribbean women travelled for pleasure each week, compared with 54 per cent of a larger sample of London women. They were likely to identify the following barriers to participation in leisure activities: having too much to do at home or at work; the cost of events and travelling to them; knowing too few people with whom to share leisure interests; it being too far to travel to events; and things being on at the wrong time. The Afro-Caribbean women were more likely than other women to take part in clubs and classes, to do voluntary work, to visit friends and relatives, and to entertain at home. The survey identified high levels of anxiety about personal safety outside the home after dark, which, coupled with a low level of car ownership because of their low incomes, keeps many women at home after dark. Forty-five per cent of the study's Afro-Caribbean respondents said that they did not go out on their own at night; 85 per cent were scared to go out after dark, and almost half felt that there were places near their homes that were unsafe even during the day-time.

Women's responses to the privations and deprivations of life in Britain can best be described in terms of a generational division between those who arrived from the West Indies after the Second World War as adults, and their daughters who have grown up here. Many of the women who came to Britain twenty or thirty years ago were committed churchgoers, for whom religion represented an enduring set of norms – a source of constancy and stability in unstable times – as well as providing opportunities for sociability without worries about financial costs or the possibility of racial harassment. Consequently the church became an important focus of leisure-time association:

> racial tensions and the pressures of a hard, long working routine made loneliness and isolation a reality for us, particularly in the fifties:
>
> 'I had no social life outside work. After the children came, I took them to church and two of them were in the choir. The only other social life was at weddings or christenings. The receptions would mostly be at people's homes.' (Bryan *et al.*, 1985, p. 31–2)

As West Indians began to move into new areas of the city and to establish communities where no ethnic churches existed, women were in the forefront of establishing these and other community organisations, to provide a focus for their common identity:

We have always been active in our community: we began by forming ourselves into small church, social and welfare groups, which were our spontaneous response to the isolation and alienation we faced when we first arrived in the Mother Country. (Bryan *et al.*, p. 124)

Activities such as these are respectable and 'safe' for women to do, and create opportunities for satisfying sociability with other members of one's cultural group, avoiding the potential embarrassment of interactions with 'outsiders' who have unfamiliar styles of communication (see Driver, 1979). They have been popular with the older generation of West Indian women, but have been rejected by many younger women in favour of more directly political or social forms of organisation. The dominant concerns of the women migrating to Britain a generation ago were to achieve a higher standard of living for their families and to rear their children successfully to adulthood – 'home-centred' goals which in some respects were little different from the aspirations of the predominantly white 'affluent workers' at a car factory studied at around the same time (Goldthorpe *et al.*, 1969). The West Indian women's children, having grown up in British society alongside white peers and been exposed to the prevailing white culture, have rather different concerns from those of their parents as a result of their own distinctive experiences. Youth culture exerts a powerful influence on black teenagers, as it does on young white people, who share a common preoccupation with its commercial products – music, entertainment, clothing and cosmetics. In employment, in education and in leisure many young black women have the same interests and topics of conversation as their white counterparts, but they share with each other a bond based on their ethnic identity, and the experiences associated with it, notably racism, which unites them and may distance them from close relationships with white peers (Sharpe, 1976; Cavendish, 1982). Long years of experiences of racism in school, at work, on the streets, in leisure venues and in media images, as well as of the institutionalised state racism of the police, the judicial system, the welfare state and immigration laws, have provided some young black women with the motivation to engage in political activism, while their parents reacted defensively and largely on a personal basis to similar affronts. Bryan, Dadzie and Scafe (1985) describe a series of political initiatives launched by black women to combat these inequities, and explain how an awareness of the racist discrimination to which all blacks are subjected has influenced black women's attempts to counter sexism, both within their relationships with men and in the wide society.

Black women experience oppression both as blacks and as women, but are able to draw on the historical tradition of the powerful matriarch, mainstay of the family, as a source of confidence and inspiration. This is not to deny black men's experience of racism, nor to romanticise the poverty, loneliness and hardships associated with lone parenthood in a society where the state offers meagre support to one-parent families. In comparison with the experiences of women from the Indian sub-continent, however, despite these difficulties women of West Indian origin in Britain appear to enjoy a higher level of autonomy about their lives and hence their leisure. Both groups are subjected to racial oppression in the form of institutionalised discrimination as well as random interpersonal acts of harassment and racial attack. One important difference between the experiences of both groups within British society lies in their orientation to the prevailing culture. For the inhabitants of Britain's former West Indian colonies, Great Britain represented a cultural homeland. Their experience of discrimination, hostility and rejection on arrival was therefore shocking and unexpected. In contrast, the various ethnic groups of Asian immigrants had no such illusions about a common, shared language, culture and life-style. Their religion, culture and language marked them off as distinctively from white British culture as did their brown skins and traditional dress, if they wore it. The possession of a distinctive cultural identity can ease the trauma of migration to an alien society by encouraging the formation of 'ghettos': a nucleus of settlers from a particular part of the homeland provides a magnet for subsequent migrants from the same district (Saifullah Khan, 1979; Rapoport *et al.*, 1982) and enables the mutual provision of informal support based on kinship or friendship to develop into the more formal provision of religious services, food shops and welfare organisations, as the community grows. However, the greater the level of social and spatial isolation of the immigrant community, and its visible distinction from the host society, the slower will be its integration into and acceptance by their society of settlement (Commission for Racial Equality, 1981), and hence the more likely is its populace to remain the target of political scapegoating and racial discrimination. The ideal, of course, would be greater respect for and celebration of ethnic and cultural diversity.

The Asian population in Britain, at about one million, is larger than the Afro-Caribbean; half of them have been born in Britain (Ballard, in Rapoport *et al.*, 1982). Like the immigration of West Indians, the large-scale migration of people from the Indian sub-continent is primarily a post-war phenomenon, and was motivated by similar reasons: a shortage of labour in Britain in the 1960s and 1970s represented prospects of economic advancement. Different patterns of family structure and sets of obligations associated with familial roles have delayed the reconstitution of extended families in Britain, a process which has been severely exacerbated by restrictive immigration legislation. The demographic structure of the Asian population in Britain is still distorted by this, with a disproportionately large number of women of child-bearing age, and hence a high birth rate, and correspondingly few elderly people. The immigrant groups have come primarily from only a few areas of the Indian sub-continent: about three-quarters of them from the Punjab, and lesser numbers from Gujerat and Bengal. Most migrants come from rural, peasant backgrounds, for whom the move to Britain represents not only immersion in an alien environment in terms of language, religion, culture and climate, but also a radical shift from a traditional agrarian lifestyle to life in an urban environment in a developed society (Saifullah Khan, 1979).

The kinship systems characteristic of rural Asian society are based on the patrifocal extended family: property transmission and place of residence are determined by the male lineage (Ballard, 1982). Households consist of a man, his sons and grandsons, their wives and unmarried daughters, who leave to join their husbands' households on marriage. These households are multi-functional and multi-generational units which live and work co-operatively at agricultural, domestic and other productive tasks. Personal preferences and autonomy are rigorously subordinated to the interests of the household unit, which is hierarchically ordered under the authority of the eldest male. Ownership of the household's property is formally vested in him, but he is expected to manage it and the family's affairs to the benefit of all. Daughters are accorded property on marriage, in the form of a dowry consisting of jewellery, clothing and household goods, which is transferred to their husband's family.

The position of women in such households is formally subordinate to men, and also to older women such as their mother-in-law. Newly married brides have little power at their disposal, and must obey the wishes of their mother-in-law. Not until the birth of children – preferably male heirs – do they earn security and status in the household. Ballard has identified the system of *purdah* (the segregation of women from men) and women's control of the domestic economy as offering partially autonomous spheres within the household 'from which it is possible to bargain both individually and collectively with men' (1982, p. 184). Wilson's (1978) book, based on interviews with Asian women living in Britain, tells a different story – of the experience of the extended family system from the perspective of its least powerful members. Male power derives from the control of property and authority within the household; a man's role is thus largely within his control. Women's success in life depends on their ability to bear male children. Their domestic labour and contribution to the productive work of the household, such as agricultural work, is taken for granted, with the rigid sexual division of labour hallowed by custom and religious laws. Although of lower status than their brothers, girls may be loved and well cared for within their own families, but this situation changes fundamentally and irrevocably on marriage. Young Muslim women are likely to marry 'cousins' living in the locality, but Hindu and Sikh women are expected by tradition to marry outside their families, and are therefore likely to move to an unfamiliar community, where nobody knows them and their status is low. This radical break with a familiar way of life is exacerbated by the tradition that the bride's parents must not accept the hospitality of the groom's parents, which makes it virtually impossible to visit her, and also by the concept of *Izzat*, or family 'honour' and 'prestige'. It is dishonourable and damaging to family pride for a new bride's parents to be confronted with incontrovertible evidence of her subjugation in her new husband's household, as this Sikh woman, recently arrived in Britain, said of her married daughter:

Yes, I wished I could see her. I felt so sad, but if I had gone there and seen her, how would I have felt? At home she was a queen, I never liked her to do the heavy jobs. There she is a slave. I know, because my life was the same. But to see her like that would hurt my feelings and hurt our *Izzat* (pride). (Wilson, 1978, p 5)

The notion that the extended family's status in the community is achieved by men but may be damaged by women's immodest or shameful behaviour (whether it be the improper observation of the rules governing dress or behaviour associated with *purdah*, or a young wife's flight from the oppression inflicted on her by her husband's family) is not specific to southern Asia.

The southern Italian traditional patterns of marriage and family relationships have interesting similarities, in the importance placed on girls' virginity, the arranged marriage system, chaperonage, the use of a dowry, and the linkage between women's sexual propriety and family honour. In both societies the strength of tradition is buttressed by religious norms to elevate the importance of women's procreative function, but the corollary of it is the powerful social pressures against girls' and women's involvement in roles and activities outside the home – except where they are a product of women's maternal and domestic roles. These constraints are particularly severe for Asian women, especially for those in Britain who are isolated from the support of female kin. As Wilson points out,

> But even in the most oppressive family and community women do have one consolation – each other's company and affection. The warmth which sisters and sisters-in-law may show for one another can cushion a woman against the harshness of her life. (p. 7)

This may be the only source of conviviality and emotional warmth for Asian women in traditional households, either in Britain or in the Indian sub-continent. The arranged marriage system does not encourage the development of intimacy between husband and wife, and they are not expected to show any overt affection for one another (Ballard, 1982). Asian women may be cut off from opportunities to form friendships with colleagues in their work-places by cultural differences, discriminatory attitudes or language barriers, or they may be prevented from entering employment by male household members' perception of it as a threat to their *Izzat* (Wilson, 1978; Cavendish, 1982).

Although there are obviously major differences in the life-styles of Asian women from different age groups, from generations of different castes and social classes, from rural or urban backgrounds, and who are more or less westernised and independent of male control within their families, there are clear cultural and religious barriers to their attainment of autonomy and sexual equality, above and beyond those faced by most white and Afro-Caribbean women. The GLC study of women's mobility in London showed their Asian women respondents to be much less likely than other women to travel alone, to engage in leisure activities away from home, to travel to and from paid work, or to use public transport (GLC, 1984). They were more likely to entertain at home and to visit friends and relatives, and were much less likely than other women to attend clubs or classes, or to do voluntary work. An important part of this focus on life and leisure within the home arises from the cultural construction of Asian femininity described earlier. Powerful reinforcement of this way of life comes from the experience of racial harassment and attack outside the relative safety of the home: these fears about personal safety, together with Asian men's reluctance to encourage women's mobility for various reasons, are reflected in the GLC's data. Even during the day-time, only half of the Asian women interviewed felt safe on British Rail trains or using the Underground, and under two-thirds felt safe walking. After dark only a very small minority of Asian women felt safe using any of these modes of transport, and 95 per cent said that they did not go out on their own after dark.

Such high levels of constraint on Asian women's leisure opportunities, especially those involving travel away from home, manifest themselves in a low level of recreational participation and make this a difficult 'target' group for policy-makers to research. Some local authorities within areas containing Asian communities have responded by developing imaginative schemes for recreational activities, publicised in native-language leaflets and offered in such a way as not to violate cultural norms. Women-only swimming sessions, with female attendants and minibus transport provided with women drivers, is one approach that has been tried. The difficulty and high cost of bringing Asian women into local authority leisure facilities makes it easy for all but strongly committed authorities to ignore this section of the community. The traditional approach to community social work, which involved identifying and working alongside local community leaders, is a recipe for further marginalising and ignoring the female half of the community, because of their invisibility in the public arena.

Elderly women's leisure patterns

The *General Household Survey* data indicate the influence of
increasing age on leisure patterns. The probability of reduced
income and deteriorating physical health with increasing age
coincided for many with a move towards home-based leisure after
retirement, which is reinforced by fears about personal safety away
from home. This has a predictable impact on the recreation habits of
elderly women. (See Mason, 1988.) Many fewer women aged over 70
gamble (other than by playing Bingo), go out for meals or drinks, do
DIY, listen to music at home, or go dancing, in comparison to
younger women's leisure activities. However, as Parker (1985, p. 21)
points out, 'there is no one pattern of life and leisure which can be
said to be typical of older women'. The same social divisions of
social class, ethnicity, employment status and family situation that
have been identified as cross-cutting with gender to shape women's
leisure opportunities, apply equally to elderly women. Patterns of
sociability and recreation established earlier in life continue so long
as the woman has the financial resources, physical health and
availability of companions to make their continuation possible.

The majority of the elderly population today are female, and the
male-female ratio widens with each successive age group. Because
the vast majority of the population marry at some stage in their
lives, and women tend to marry older men, the experience of many
elderly women is widowhood and the end of their 'couple'
relationship on which so much leisure activity is predicated.
However, despite this demographic evidence about their numerical
domination, older women continue to be neglected in studies of
ageing and retirement: it is assumed that generalisations about the
experiences of men apply with equal validity to women, or that such
major life transitions as retirement will 'have relatively little impact
on women since the work role is less salient for them that it is for
men' (Jerrome, 1984). The assumptions persist unchallenged in the
literature that work is a 'central life interest' for men but not for
women, and that family roles and domestic activities, which
continue beyond retirement for women, cushion them from the
deprivation of status, income, social relationships and a temporal
structure to the day which employment provided. Jerrome
challenges these perceptions, showing how her sample of
middle-class older women employed the social skills acquired in

employment or through participation in organisations to establish or develop friendships with other women. Single-sex groups, whether based on private friendships, kin networks or voluntary associations, offer a forum for relaxed sociability where marital status becomes irrelevant, and the women are actively engaged in constructing their own social lives, rather than being reluctant participants in activities organised by others on their behalf: 'lunch clubs or other activities for the elderly are viewed with scorn and horror' (Jerrome, p. 13).

A large 1977 study of people aged over 75, two-thirds of whom were women, also found a low level of popularity of clubs for the elderly among their target population (Abrams, 1978). Only 13 per cent of the over-75s interviewed were members, and they were significantly more likely to be living alone. Social clubs not just for the elderly, and religious organisations (such as church, chapel or synagogue groups) were more popular, especially for elderly women and those living alone. Three-fifths of the women aged over 75 lived alone, and two-fifths lived with others, usually their partner and/or children. For both groups passive leisure occupations were the most important way of spending their free time: watching television, listening to the radio, reading and 'just resting' accounted on average for eight hours per day (Abrams, 1980). Only a third of respondents had been for a walk on the day preceding the interview, and physical mobility problems were a major barrier for many of the sample. A quarter of the women did knitting and sewing; not very many did other home-based pastimes. Apart from mobility difficulties associated with poor health, which applied to significant numbers of both men and women, whether living alone or with others, there is evidence that the leisure experiences of elderly women are circumscribed by poverty to a greater extent than those of other segments of the population. Only 2 per cent of the older women living alone had access to a car, compared with 15 per cent of all those in this age group. They were also less likely to have a washing machine, refrigerator, colour television or telephone.

Evidence about the impact of age on travel patterns from the GLC study provides some confirmation of the results of Abrams' study (GLC, 1985). Over three-quarters of the women aged over 75 did some walking each week (10 per cent fewer than 'all women'), but they were very much less likely to use expensive forms of transport such as private cars, British Rail and Underground trains, or taxis. Elderly women's main reason for travelling was to do 'essential shopping', but two-fifths of their journeys were 'for pleasure'. This is less frequent than the leisure-related travel patterns of younger women; home-based activities such as home or garden tasks, hobbies, television and entertaining at home are done more often. More women aged over 75 than others felt that their social life was limited and that mobility problems were partly responsible for this.

As for the Afro-Caribbean and Asian women described earlier, elderly women's fears for their personal safety outside the home were a major constraint on their participation in leisure activities away from home. Seventy per cent reported never going out on their own after dark, and even in the day-time only one-third of them felt safe using British Rail or Underground trains, and two-thirds felt safe walking. Buses – a frequent local and inexpensive means of transport and the one most often used apart from walking – were perceived as the safest form of travel.

Conclusion

The leisure activities which women do most frequently and on which they spend the majority of their free time are those that can be done at home; that can be done in the bits of time left over from doing other things, or that can easily be interrupted if necessary. The activities do not require expensive equipment or facilities other than those readily available; they rarely challenge stereotyped assumptions about the 'nature' of women as wives, mothers and daughters; and they are safe, and demand little expenditure of energy. In short, women's patterns of recreation are entirely predictable, given the structural and normative context of their lives. It is therefore important, when studying women's leisure, to locate its analysis within a broad framework that is capable of explaining the links between their position in the wider society and their patterns of recreational activity.

5

Work and leisure

Introduction

This book began with a critique of the androcentric approach to the sociology of leisure which dominated the discipline during the 1970s. The traditional distinction made both in leisure studies and in popular culture between 'work' and 'leisure' established a polarisation between them which, as we have come to recognise, has little to offer in advancing our understanding of most women's leisure experiences and, indeed, is hardly relevant for those sizeable sections of the male population not in full-time paid employment. Since then a far more sophisticated set of theoretical analyses has developed of the interactions of social structural and normative forces which influence people's leisure behaviour. These have been informed by contributions from different, often sharply opposed, perspectives and disciplines such as Marxism, feminism and cultural studies, which have challenged the prevailing orthodoxy established by social geographers and pluralists within leisure studies; and also by the synthesis of empirical material from a catholic range of sources, drawing on both qualitative and quantitative data. The outcome of this protracted debate has been a measure of agreement about the need to analyse leisure patterns in relation to people's position in the labour market using theoretical models which recognise the complex interplay of relevant forces. Simple assertions about the influence of a person's occupational culture on their leisure patterns, which represented advanced thinking in the 1970s (for example, Salaman, 1974), have been superseded by studies which use interdisciplinary perspectives to link social structural, cultural and political factors as pertinent in analysing leisure (such as Dixey and Talbot, 1982; Clarke and Critcher, 1985).

The purpose of this chapter is to explore evidence of the implications of paid and unpaid work for women's leisure experiences. This will not be done in any deterministic sense, suggesting that women in a specific occupational category or at the same point in their life-course inevitably have similar recreational patterns. Rather, the aim is to explore the kinds of constraints and opportunities for women's leisure that are associated with their various relationships to the labour market. Clearly women's own paid employment will influence the time available to them for leisure, their disposable income, the availability of leisure companions, and the scope for 'having a laugh' with workmates on the job. But even within a single workplace the varied circumstances of women employees will influence their orientation to leisure: their domestic situation, age group, ethnic identity and position in the organisation will all have a bearing on what leisure means to them and its place in their lives as a whole.

'Work' for women however, is, not just a matter of their paid employment. Beyond the manifest impact of their own jobs on their leisure opportunities lies the less tangible influence of other kinds of work: unpaid domestic labour; the care of dependants – children, male partners, elderly relatives – and support of various kinds for male partners in their employment. For many women their domestic labour and childcare responsibilities occupy many more waking hours than most employees spend on their jobs. The increasing proportion of very elderly people in the population in many Western societies, coupled with prevailing ideologies about women's roles as carers, means that the care of elderly dependants could come to occupy more woman-years than the care of small children by the turn of the century, as the birthrate decreases. Women who have paid jobs as well as primary responsibility for housekeeping typically find themselves doing a 'double shift' of paid and unpaid labour, in addition to providing support of other kinds to members of the household as part of their pivotal caring role.

The impact of women's employment on their leisure

Paid employment influences women's leisure in a variety of ways. Women's own full-time or part-time employment consumes time which may otherwise be potentially available for leisure. Although the legitimacy of taking time from domestic work to spend on personal leisure is in practice problematic, it does provide women with an independent income, opportunities to develop social contacts at work, and some notional entitlement, at least, to autonomous leisure. In the Sheffield study three-fifths of the women employed full-time felt that they had too little time for leisure, but the other two-fifths were satisfied with the amount of free time available to them. More of the part-time employed women were satisfied – over half of them – but two-fifths still felt deprived of sufficient free time (Green, Hebron and Woodward, 1987b, 1987c). These differences as we will see later, are largely attributable to variations in the other commitments women have in their lives apart from their employment. Young, single, employed women, who see most of their waking hours other than those spent at work as potentially available for leisure, are infinitely more privileged in this respect than working mothers with small children, whose domestic commitments have to be fitted into this time left over from paid work.

The burden of this 'double shift' of employment and housework for wives, and particularly mothers, comes out clearly from a number of recent studies of women in factory employment. Sue Sharpe (1984) interviewed over a hundred women, most of them white, living in various cities in England and Scotland. Sixty per cent of them worked part-time and forty per cent full-time, predominantly in working-class jobs. One in five were lone parents. Many women's jobs are boring, physically or mentally exhausting, repetitive, alienating, and badly paid, offering little possibility of intrinsic rewards or job satisfaction. Ruth Cavendish's (1982) study of women workers in a motor components factory and Anna Pollert's (1981) study of women workers in a tobacco factory likewise graphically show the tedium of unskilled factory work. Sallie Westwood's (1984) account of female shopfloor culture in a hosiery factory describes the tyranny of the measured day-work payment system which, like piecework, exerts an unremitting pressure on the workers to maintain high rates of productivity in order to maintain their wage levels. Both she and Pollert point out that, contrary to the stereotyped view of women workers, their primary motivation for doing this work was, just like men's, their weekly wage packet. The women's position in the labour market restricted their 'choice' of working to relatively poorly paid factory jobs, in which they were seen by management as 'factors of production'. Obviously work for some men also gives them little opportunity for the development of self-respect and new skills, but the differential position of men and women in the labour market means that the constraints that lead people into this kind of work apply to many more women than men. Also, as Sharpe points out, few men have the prime responsibility for running a home and looking after other family members, as well as their paid jobs. Shopping, cooking and cleaning have to be fitted in around work, leaving working women with little free time and even less energy for their own leisure.

The way in which women's paid work and domestic responsibilities are fitted together varies according to the nature and location of their jobs, their working hours, and the number and ages of their children. Some of Sharpe's respondents talked about the exhausting nature of their jobs: doing factory work on piece-rates, collecting train tickets, and teaching. The tiredness associated with doing their paid work is exacerbated by their domestic obligations – the need to produce meals and clean clothes, and to look after children, and the burden of responsibility for making sure that family members' various needs are met. The pressures to conform to the demands of the paid job by being 'a good worker', as well as striving to maintain the same high standards of housework and childcare as full-time housewives, leaves pitifully little opportunity for leisure during the working week. As one Sheffield mother, in a study of women working part-time, said:

> This is why you don't want to do things at night. By the time you've worked a full day and you've come home and you've cooked a meal, washed up, done your bits and bobs, there's always something to do. (Green and Parry, 1982)

The working day of the women tobacco factory workers studied by Pollert typically began with some housework at 5.30 a.m. or 6 a.m. before they left home to get the bus to the factory. Many spent their lunch-hour doing shopping, and after paid work finished at 4.30 p.m. came more shopping, cooking and housework. An hour spent watching television was their weekday leisure, before bedtime and the next working day. Not surprisingly, Pollert notes:

> The strain showed. Women aged 30 looked 40: their skin pale, tired and drawn. Little surprise they had no intention of 'working for ever'. (Pollert, 1981, p. 112)

A 1986 study of shiftworkers found that those who were married women had least leisure: their non-work time occurred in parts of the day when family and friends were not available for sociability, and it was swallowed up by housework (Aubrey *et al.*, 1986).

Women's employment patterns create particular difficulties in relation to childcare. Even 'normal' childcare arrangements are for many women complicated, fragile, privately-organised systems, because of the poor provision of facilities by either employers or the state in Britain. These arrangements are frequently liable to disruption, because of children's and carers' illnesses, transport problems, bad weather, teachers' strikes, appointments with clinics, doctors and dentists, and other kinds of not uncommon 'exceptional circumstances'. The younger the woman's children, the more acute these problems of juggling the conflicting demands of being 'a good worker' and 'a good mother' are likely to be. In the absence of sufficient formally organised childcare places which meet the real needs of children and their working parents, most working mothers of pre-school children use childminders or female relatives to look after them during the day-time. Husbands' presence at home in the evenings enable many women to do part-time jobs, but such work is commonly badly paid and exploitative because employers realise that their workers have little alternative. A woman interviewed for Dixey and Talbot's study of bingo pointed out that it not only provided women with an important form of recreation outside the home, but was also a major employer of local women:

> Because it's at a time when the husbands can watch the kids, until they can get something that pays better because it's not very well paid. They don't keep their staff long, but it's an ideal going back to work job when you've been at home for a while having kids. Well it's slave market really. They know that women are desperate for the money. It's like these evening cleaning jobs. They know they are desperate for a bit of extra money so they think 'We'll pay the least we can get away with; somebody will take it'. (Dixey and Talbot, 1982, p. 25)

In Sharpe's study, over half of the mothers with children under school age used husbands, mothers, mothers-in-law and other relatives or friends to look after their children while they were working, or they kept their children with them. The advantages of keeping childcare 'within the family' are several: the children are with 'someone they know', which is considered important. If a person is taking care of the children for love, rather than for money, mothers' guilt is assuaged about neglecting their children to do paid work outside the home. This kind of arrangement does not cost money, although it may entail costs of other kinds. If women's paid work is done while their men partners are at home, and hence are available for childcare, there is scant time left for families to enjoy leisure together. Many women in this position see very little of their young children during the working week. Those who use the services of their female relatives for childcare may find that this incurs reciprocal obligations of other sorts which cut into precious free time, for example doing their housework, or being expected to invite them for meals.

For women who find the double burden of full-time employment and domestic responsibilities to be physically exhausting and to leave them no time for themselves, part-time work can appear to be the desirable option. As Sharpe points out, 'it seems to offer the best of both worlds' (p. 187) – extra income for the family on top of the male breadwinner's wage, and a break from the monotony and isolation of the home, which should still leave women with time for their domestic and family commitments, and leisure too. In Britain, more than in other advanced Western societies, large numbers of women have entered the labour force as part-time employees since Myrdal and Klein's pioneering analysis, *Women's Two Roles: Home and Work* (1956), recommended it as an ideal solution to the role conflicts of mothers who wanted to or needed to work. But there are hidden costs to this form of employment. Hakim (1987) demonstrates that the labour force is divided into two halves: the full-time, permanent workers and the part-time, maybe temporary 'flexibles'. Fifty per cent of women workers come within the 'flexibles' compared with only 25 per cent of male workers. This prompts Walby (1983) to ask the following questions:

> So is this flexibility gendered? Is the core masculine and the periphery feminine? Whose flexibility is it? Does part-time work simultaneously meet the needs of women, employers and husbands or merely one of these groups?

The answers to these questions have consequences for other areas of life, not least in terms of the effect on access to leisure time. Beechey (1987, p. 213) has argued that the nature of part-time work in Britain has a female bias to an extent that is unmatched in other advanced capitalist countries:

There is considerably more male part-time employme
capitalist countries (Japan, the United States and
instance) and more part-time employment among yo
(the United States for example).

But newly available international evidence demc
relationship between levels of women's employment and part-time
working is more complicated than 1970s studies of women's work
suggested. In their most recent work, which includes a comparison
of part-time working patterns across OECD countries, Beechey and
Perkins (1987, p. 41) state that: 'At 94.3 per cent the United
Kingdom had the highest proportion of women part-timers of any
country in 1981', but they note that Germany and Denmark follow
closely behind. So although other advanced capitalist countries have
comparably high levels of part-time working, the degree to which
that work is gender-segregated is related to a variety of factors,
including state policies and cultural norms about the nature of
women's work.

However, the seductive possibilities of part-time work for women
with domestic responsibilities may not be matched by the reality.
Part-time work is predominantly 'women's work', and is likely to be
the most exploitative pattern of employment in terms of low wages,
poor working conditions, little job security, and exclusion from
'fringe benefits' such as pensions, subsidised meals, and so on. Part-
time workers are often the least visible, most marginalised and least
unionised members of large organisations, and are even more
difficult to organise collectively to try to improve their conditions if
they work in small enterprises, as many do. The difficulties of
arranging substitute childcare during school holidays force many
women to leave their part-time work, and to look for another job as
the new school term begins. This behaviour reinforces employers'
perceptions of such women workers as merely 'a reserve army of
labour', and weakens still further their tenuous foothold in the
labour market.

The greatest problem for most working women, whether full-time
or part-time, in restricting their leisure time is the unequal division
of labour within the home. Notwithstanding current media interest
in the emergence of the non-sexist 'New Man', who allegedly takes
an equal share in childcare and domestic work, there is a powerful
consensus from a wide range of studies that these responsibilities are

almost universally seen as women's, rather than shared ones. Certainly, significant changes have taken place over the last thirty years in norms about male participation and childcare, and in terms of the tasks which husbands and fathers now do. This can be seen if the studies discussed here are compared with ethnographic accounts of the domestic division of labour in various British communities in the 1950s (see for example, Slater and Woodside, 1951, and Dennis, Henriques and Slaughter, 1969). Two of Sharpe's interviewees described the changes in their husbands' contribution to the domestic routine associated with their own return to work:

> He never used to share with the housework a lot . . . But now he's making his own tea at night when I go out, he gets the bairns to bed, and he has something to eat, and when I come home the dishes are washed that he's used, which he never used to do before, and he has the kettle boiled for us, he's a bit more helpful, y'know.

> I used to do everything in the house. He could just come in from work, sit down, and I'd bring his tea, a cooked tea, he didn't have to do a thing, but now we're both working, if I'm tired I say, 'Oh Chris, I can't be bothered.' 'Right, I'll do it', he'll say, 'we're both working, we've both got to do what's what in the house.' The main thing I've got to do on a weekend is the Sunday dinner because he does all the housework and everything. He helps out a lot in the house since we've both been working, it's been better altogether.' (Sharpe, 1984, pp. 175–6)

Men, too, recognised these social changes:

> Stan (*chargehand*): All this women's lib stuff is stupid, because I help my wife at home and most men do. Women don't have anything to complain about. (Pollert, 1981, p. 114)

However, closer examination of what tasks men actually do in the home, how often they are done and to what standard, in relation to the totality of responsibility for the management of housekeeping and the care of household members, reveals a rather different picture:

> And with most women it became apparent that 'sharing' meant a limited delegation of specific tasks to their husbands, while they bore the *responsibility* for the endless, *undefined*, niggling work. And even this division often broke down – the women had high standards, the men lacked the training and skill. (Pollert, pp. 114–15, original emphasis)

Hunt (1980) describes how 'women are trained and conditioned to accept responsibility for household order and cleanliness'. All the women she studied had higher housework standards than their husbands. Sharpe concurs, pointing out that men's ostensible incapability of performing certain tasks arises from their 'cultivated ineptitude'. Many men partners could do certain tasks, and did do them if their wives were not around to do them, but changes in patterns of leaving for work and coming home were often by default associated with a redistribution of domestic tasks. This seems to be one reason for the minimal change in the sexual division of domestic labour which seems to accompany women's entry to part-time work, especially if it is done during the man's worktime, and hence causes no visible difference in terms of her presence in the home. Non-working mothers with employed husbands usually take responsibility for most of the housework and childcare, and this is generally seen as equitable. According to Sharpe's interviewees, if women are employed full-time it is generally considered that fathers should help a lot, if not equally; and where they work part-time, that fathers should help proportionately. However, this does not happen in practice, and the nature and extent of men's participation in childcare depended much more on their own attitudes than on their wives' working patterns.

An Australian study of working mothers found that the husbands of women employed full-time did, on average, a third less housework than their wives, and the domestic workload of women working part-time was about the same as that of the full-time housewives (Harper and Richards, 1979). Other studies have similarly found that married women's employment, whether part-time and temporary or professional and permanent, is not associated with any significant redistribution of housework tasks or domestic responsibilities from the traditional sexual division of labour (see for example Young and Willmott, 1973; Edgell, 1980; Hunt, 1980; Deem, 1986a).

However, paid work does not consist of all disadvantages and constraints for women's leisure. It has important advantages for women's sense of self-worth and their authority within the household. Earning their own income confers a measure of economic independence on women, giving them a more powerful voice in negotiations and decision-making within the home, including decisions about their own leisure. As one of Hunt's informants, who was financially dependent on her husband, said:

> I've never had pocket money. I've gone out with my husband either because I've got no choice, you know, I've gone out with him for a night out because I've got no money to go anywhere so I've got to go where *he* wants to go, or I've suggested somewhere and he's come with me, but he's had to pay, like. (Hunt, 1980, original emphasis)

This negative impact on their own leisure of women's financial dependence on men partners was borne out in the Sheffield study (Green, Hebron and Woodward, 1987b).

Even if the low level of women's wages means that any transformation in the marital relationship takes place more at the symbolic level, rather than generating revolutionary changes in actual domestic practices, the psychological implications of financial independence for women should not be underestimated.

> Even a small income from a part-time job may allow at least some glimpse of an alternative to permanent dependency within marriage. Simply being aware of this potential is as important as the ability to realise it, as it can make women more confident and assertive and reduce the feelings of powerlessness that can be induced by total financial dependency. (Sharpe, 1984, p. 76)

This is borne out by research by Land (1983) and Pahl (1984) into patterns of financial decision-making within the household unit, which identifies the links between wage-earning and power.

If access to even a small earned income of one's own makes such a significant difference to the perceived balance of power within a marriage, what are the experiences of women in professional careers or management, who earn high salaries? Studies of wives in 'dual career families', and of women managers and doctors, tend not to address the issue of women's leisure specifically (Rapoport and Rapoport, 1976; Cooper and Davidson, 1982; Lorber, 1984), but their profiles of these women's lives enable us to draw conclusions about the impact of their occupational and domestic commitments on leisure opportunities. The study of women managers by Cooper and Davidson identified the social pressures on unmarried women to become 'workaholics' in order to prove themselves worthy of promotion to senior level in a male-dominated work environment. The married women, particularly those with children, experienced guilt and overwork at trying to meet the conflicting demands imposed on them by their job, their husband, motherhood and housekeeping. They spent more time on childcare and household tasks than male managers did, with little support from employers or the state, and even sometimes from their partners. The pressures of striving to be Superwoman left very little time for leisure.

Paid work enhances women's feelings of self-respect and power to influence domestic decision-making, it provides women with an independent identity separate from being someone's wife or mother, and – in a society still dominated by the Protestant work ethic – it can confer the right to some free time, should the woman wish to press this claim, in a way which the roles of housewife and mother do not. Another major advantage of paid work is the possibilities it affords for sociability and close friendships with other women. As Sharpe points out (1984, p. 228), the social relationships of the workplace and its 'culture' are particularly attractive to women returning to paid work from the isolated role of full-time housewife, but women of all ages and from a variety of occupational backgrounds have been found to identify them as the most positive aspects of their employment. Hard, monotonous factory work can be made bearable by sharing with workmates fantasies of escape to a better life (Pollert, 1981), by helping and supporting other women 'on the job' (Cavendish, 1982), and, above all, by maintaining a friendly interest in colleagues' private lives (Sharpe, 1984; West-wood, 1983).

The various studies of women's cultures on the factory floor identify the significance of workplace friendships and 'having a laugh' in making work tolerable and, at times, enjoyable.

> Laura, too, emphasised the importance of the people at the factory: 'It's the people who make StitchCo. You're never bored because there's always something happening and the other girls are so friendly we're always having a "laff". I really missed it when I went to do that nanny job.'

> The things that were 'happening' varied from scurrilous gossip to organised pranks, but they were given life through the network of friends. There were no 'laffs' to be had on your own: bunking off to the toilets, spending too much time in the coffee bar made no sense if it was an individual activity; there was no way to organise a prank without your mates or to have a laff at a pornie picture or a coarse joke. The material base for all of these was the friendship group. (Westwood, 1984, p. 90–1)

Given the poor wages available for women's manual labour and minimal prospects of advancement, these work friendships may militate against women's job mobility – especially if the working hours and location fit in well with women's domestic commitments – and they provide valued opportunities for women to enjoy 'leisure' at work. Both Wimbush's (1986) study and the Sheffield study found evidence of women's employment enriching their leisure in the form of events away from home with workmates – opportunities generated by the wider range of social contacts provided by work, access to personal spending money from women's own wages, and a stronger sense of entitlement to such leisure. Wimbush also points out that employment opens up new 'spaces' for leisure in women's lives, such as reading on the bus to work and chatting with workmates during breaks.

Even though few studies of women's employment explicitly say so, the evidence clearly shows the impact of women's paid work on their opportunities for leisure, especially for married and cohabiting women and women who are mothers, because of the prevailing unequal division of domestic labour and responsibilities. The 'double shift' of full-time employment and domestic work leaves many women with pitifully little time and energy for leisure in its normally accepted sense – of participation in recreational activities.

The impact of male partners' employment on women's leisure

The unequal domestic division of labour which, as we have seen, makes major inroads into the non-work time of employed women, has a similarly significant bearing on the lives of partners of employed men, especially if they are 'housewives'. Paid work has long been seen as a normal and even desirable 'central life interest' for men, especially middle-class men (Sofer, 1970; Pahl and Pahl, 1971; Edgell, 1980), whereas prevailing norms assume the home and the family to be women's primary concerns. The role of the 'good wife' is to create a happy family life within the social and geographical environment predicated upon her partner's employment. It is conventionally viewed as being in the family's interests and hence the woman's own, in material terms at least, for her to support him in his work.

Not surprisingly, there is very little published research which claims to study the impact of men's working patterns on women's leisure, but there is a considerable accumulation of relevant material that can be derived from a careful reading of studies about the relationship between men's employment and their family relationships, as well as studies of 'family life' in various social contexts. A particularly useful source of material is Finch's *Married to the Job: Wives' Incorporation in Men's Work* (1983), which is one of the few studies that focuses on women's experiences of life in relation to constraints associated with their partners' employment. Finch begins by pointing out, as others have done, that:

> A man's work imposes a set of structures upon his wife's life, which consequently constrain her choices about the living of her own life, and set limits upon what is possible for her. These structures are, of course – both analytically and in experience – part of the more general structure into which, characteristically in our culture, a woman enters when she marries. (p. 2)

Variations in men partners' working patterns and conditions, such as shiftwork, trips away from the home area, working from home, unpredictable hours of work or being 'on call', as well as the outcome of interpersonal negotiations about how to deal with them, influence women's lives by constraining and structuring their routines and freedom of choice. Dominant ideologies about gender roles within marriage legitimate this: the role of 'chief breadwinner' is accorded primacy in the domestic arrangements of most households, and takes precedence over the interests and preferences of other household members, for sound economic reasons. This state of affairs is buttressed by cultural accretions which, since the separation of the home from the workplace occurred after the Industrial Revolution, have vested in male employment powerful notions about 'masculinity' and 'adult status' which have enhanced the emotional attachment between men and their jobs way beyond the instrumental goal of earning a living. This concept is no mere figment of the industrial sociologist's imagination. Although some studies do suggest a weakening attachment of certain groups of male workers to their jobs and to the Protestant work ethic which legitimated and promoted this attachment (see Veal, 1987), powerful contrary evidence comes from studies of the experience of male unemployment, as we shall see later.

The impact of men's employment on their women partners' lives is by no means a uniform and entirely predictable phenomenon. A considerable part of the labour market inequalities between men and women may be attributable to the patterns of norms and values outlined above, especially married women's higher rates of part-time and low-paid employment than other groups of workers. However, individuals' responses to the situation in which they find themselves is shaped, rather than determined, by their circumstances. In their study of managers and their wives Pahl and Pahl write:

> the interaction between work and home cannot be simply along a one-way street, with the family at the receiving end. A man may be a manager when he is at work; when he is at home, as husband and father, different influences affect him. (Pahl and Pahl, 1971, p. 111)

As Finch points out, even the 'greediest' of male occupations in terms of the demands it imposes on members of the family elicits a range of responses from wives. The most extreme example of a husband's job constraining his wife's as well as his own daily life is the resident British Rail crossing gatekeeper! Here the non-negotiable requirement that the gates should be opened and closed at fixed times, punctuated mealtimes, household tasks and even sleep, as well as imposing severe constraints on both partners' leisure. Other studies reveal the scope for members of occupational communities, especially in rural areas, to exercise social control over wives' leisure, because of the visibility of the women's behaviour outside the home in the 'public' arena, for example the English mining community studied in *Coal Is Our Life* (Dennis *et al.*, 1969) and the Australian farming town studied by Dempsey (1987). In other occupations there is scope for negotiation about how aspects of the 'spillover' of men's work into the family domain should be managed, but underpinning such negotiations are deeply held norms, which appear to be fairly consistent across social groups, about the 'proper' role of the wife in relation to her partner's job. The economic value of this unpaid domestic work provided by the wife, to service the needs of the male worker and to rear his children as the next generation of wage-labourers, is now recognised by social scientists, if not by employers and politicians, as benefiting capitalism. The precise form taken by this 'servicing' role, above and beyond the provision of daily domestic services, seems to vary between occupational and social class groups, and over time.

The conventional wisdom of the 1960s was that middle-class men with management careers in large organisations were willing to subordinate their family's interests to those of the firm in relation to working time versus time spent with the family, and the frequency of household relocation. This was justified by the men concerned to themselves, to their families, and to society at large in terms of the material benefits associated with career achievements. By the 1970s evidence was available to confirm that, although the managers studied were still working long hours, there was much less uncritical acceptance of the ideology that the man's career should take precedence over family life. Pahl and Pahl wrote in 1971 about the managers they studied:

> How can they say (as most of them do) that they are working hard for their wives and families when the very fact of working prevents them from being with the people for whom they are said to be working? None of the managers complained about the burden of work – although of course their wives did – are we then to assume that they enjoy it? (p. 257–8)

They found evidence of widespread dissatisfaction amongst the wives interviewed about the extent of their husbands' work commitment, although it was felt to be improper and disloyal to express these opinions, especially to an outsider. A number of the managers studied by Sofer (1970) also voiced serious reservations about committing themselves any further to their companies, in terms of hours worked and moving house, because of potential conflicts between their families' welfare and their own leisure interests.

Since the early 1970s there have been significant social changes in relation to employment – in women's opportunities for education and training, in the relative positions of men and women in the labour market and in (some) employers' expectations about their women employees, and within households. Patterns of marriage, cohabitation, fertility and divorce have undergone major changes, and traditional patterns of the domestic division of labour are coming under private and public scrutiny. How far these are issues which merely exercise a thoughtful section of the press, or whether they do represent a real and major shift in individuals' behaviour, is a matter of debate. However, it is certain that the previous assumptions of sociologists, based on information from their middle-class respondents in the 1950s and 1960s, that middle-class women's best strategy for a comfortable and contended life lay in marriage to a manager or a professional worker, are no longer valid.

During recent years studies of the impact of men partners' employment on the structure and quality of women's lives have broadened the scope of analysis beyond just the middle classes, and have identified a series of forms which this relationship can take. The stereotypical manager's wife, as 'gregarious, confident and extroverted; greedy for material goods and ambitious for her husband, fostering his career in whatever way she can' (Pahl and Pahl, p. 176), has been supplanted by a complex categorisation of the meshing of men's work and women's lives. Further studies of the wives of men in middle-class occupations have taken us beyond the confines of the 'executive's wife' model, revealing the varied forms of support to their partners' careers provided by the wives of doctors, scientists and academics, clergy, civil servants, diplomats, policemen and army officers (Cain, 1973; Callan, 1975; Mitchell, 1975; Edgell, 1980; Fowlkes, 1980; Gerber, 1983; and Finch, 1983). The different forms of 'servicing' by wives that are taken-for-granted benefits of employing married men in these occupations are explored in detail by Finch. She cites Papenek's analysis of the 'vicarious achievement' in relation to their partners' careers obtained by middle-class women, as they perform secretarial services, entertain formal visitors, offer social work skills and engage in community activities, all of which are 'structurally generated' as part of the middle-class wife's expected role.

Other forms of the 'incorporation' of wives' time and labour into their husbands' work hark back to the time before the Industrial Revolution when productive work mainly took place within the household. Farmers and bakers (Delphy, 1977) and couples who run small businesses (Scase and Goffee, 1982) may experience exactly the same lack of spatial or temporal division between 'work' and 'play', and the associated problems or advantages in reconciling the demands of work, family interests and leisure, as small-scale entrepreneurs did a century and a half ago (Hall, 1982).

Despite the passage of time and an ostensible shift in public attitudes (and perhaps in private behaviour) about the work/home relationship in recent years, many of the issues which Finch identifies as constraining wives' freedom to have jobs in their own right or to enjoy leisure are broadly similar to those highlighted by the mangers' wives studied by Pahl and Pahl (1971). Women's free time is severely constrained by their men partner's working patterns and the asymmetrical division of domestic responsibilities, which leaves women with the primary responsibility for housework and childcare, and the care of elderly relatives. This 'spillover' of the husband's work commitments into home life is not just a matter of their physical absence, but also has important emotional, social and psychological connotations. The wives of men in occupations with a high public profile may experience 'vicarious contamination', which identifies a particular (unpaid) public role for them, such as the wives of ambassadors and clergymen, or which presents a barrier to their own sociability with others outside this occupation, such as the wives of policemen or prison officers. Some occupations involve the use of the home as a semi-public place for business and other transactions, for example, farmers, clergymen and where businesses or practices are run at or from home. Even if the wives have no formal involvement in their husbands' work, this pattern imposes the burden on them of having to maintain higher domestic standards, since the home is permanently liable to public scrutiny, and makes access to unambiguous leisure time problematic. The expectation that wives will deal with telephone calls and visitors and provide hospitality encroaches on their autonomy and privacy. Finch points out that these constraints are a much greater burden on wives than would appear merely from the time spent on this kind of work: the normative assumptions that wives will automatically provided this labour to support their husbands' work, whether it is recognised and remunerated (as for General Practitioners' wives who work as their receptionists), or is merely expected by custom and practice (as for the wives of military officers, diplomats, Members of Parliament or clergymen) severely constrain their own opportunities for work and leisure. This socially structured invisibility of wives' participation in their partners' work, and the fact that much of the work is done within the 'private' sphere of the home, obscure its real value to the men concerned and to their employers.

Unemployment and women's leisure

Recent studies of the experience of unemployment highlight the constraints imposed by poverty on people's freedom of choice. Customary patterns and practices about diet, mobility and leisure come under close scrutiny when money is in short supply, whereas those in more affluent circumstances take such things for granted. Fourteen per cent of the women surveyed in the Sheffield study had husbands who were unemployed, and this group was selected for detailed study at the interview stage to find out how their leisure experiences had changed. Nearly nine out of ten reported lack of money to be a problem in relation to their leisure, compared with under six out of ten of the women with partners in employment. The unemployed men's wives spent less on leisure activities than other women, and were much more likely to have cut back on leisure spending in the previous year. These economies particularly restricted couple-based leisure activities outside the home. Many favourite leisure activities had to be abandoned or were done much less frequently now, because the cost of doing them could not be managed within a severely restricted budget. Dancing, bingo, and even an occasional drink at the local pub with adult children had to be curtailed. Although in theory one round of drinks could be made to last the whole evening, the humiliation of not being able to reciprocate by 'paying their call' in return for drinks bought by friends or relatives could be sufficient to prevent such trips altogether:

> I don't want to go out. If I can't pay for anything, I don't want to go out, so that's how it is. (Wife of unemployed man)

A couple of women in their sixties commented on the social isolation that results from being deprived access because of poverty to the only significant forum for sociability in their locality – the pub or the club. For younger wives of unemployed men, who had small children, the impact of a restricted budget bore particularly hard on their participation as a couple in leisure activities outside the home. Their need for baby-sitters, who have to be paid in cash or kind, made the opportunity for going out together even more remote and infrequent than for other mothers of young children. Women in the survey with unemployed partners were less likely than others to use baby-sitters, used them much less frequently, and were more likely to use relatives for baby-sitting, who, presumably, would not expect any cash payment for this service.

In the previous section we considered the impact of men's employment patterns in structuring women's leisure opportunities. If husbands do not have paid employment they will not have work habits that impinge on their wives' free time and, in theory if not in practice, therefore have much more time at their disposal for sharing domestic tasks and childcare. Male unemployment could thus be a potent liberating force for their wives' leisure. There is some evidence from the Sheffield survey to support this: the wives of unemployed men were more likely to report having more than five hours' free time on weekdays in the day time and the evening than other women, and – unlike other women – never had their planned leisure activities disrupted by problems related to their husband. They did not, however, seem to find it any easier than other women to set aside time for their own leisure. Evidence from other studies suggests that the presence of an unemployed husband at home can be a mixed blessing. The older couples interviewed in the Sheffield study enjoyed walks and joint outings, spending much more time together in this way than had been possible when each partner was in employment, but the young women who were full-time housewives could find their existing networks of social relationships severely disrupted by the unaccustomed presence of their male partners. McKee and Bell, in their study of the households of unemployed men with young families, found that:

> in some cases wives' social ties and interaction patterns could be devastated. Wives could be restricted in their contact with other female friends. This seemed to cut both ways: friends could stay away, not wanting to intrude on marital privacy, *or* wives were discouraged by husbands from pursuing an independent social life.
> Even when female friends continued to call, despite the unemployed husband's presence, the quality of interaction could be affected and some women reported that conversations were inhibited. Husbands served as 'gooseberries' on these occasions. Some husbands themselves confessed that they found it difficult to accept their wives' separate day-time social life and put themselves in direct competition with her friends and interests. Wives were torn between keeping husbands company and sustaining former bonds and routines.

They observe that it became clear to them in the course of their research

> that men and women have differential access to community support with women having more ready-made links with neighbours and kin and sometimes being better placed than men. However, male unemployment can herald a change for the worse and enforce isolation not just on the husband but on the couple. (McKee and Bell, 1983)

It is not only women's social relationships with friends and neighbours that can be disrupted by the constant presence of an unemployed partner: their roles as housewives and mothers may also be affected. McKee and Bell point out how much more time-consuming shopping and the preparation of meals become when these have to be managed on a low income, especially as shopping trips are likely to be done on foot and fitted around other domestic commitments and childcare. The day-time presence of a husband can force a modification of normal household routines. Beds cannot be made or bedrooms cleaned if a husband is sleeping late, and husbands' mere physical presence 'in the way' of getting domestic tasks done, as well as the extra mouth which consumes meals and drinks and generates extra washing up, may well enlarge rather than diminish the magnitude of the housewife's tasks. Both McKee and Bell's women respondents and those in the Sheffield study voiced complaints about unemployed partners' do-it-yourself projects generating extra mess in the home, and unfinished jobs were a source of stress and marital conflict. Some women felt their standards as housewives and mothers were more exposed to scrutiny, and hence to possible criticism, when husbands spent considerably more time in the home. McKee and Bell point out:

> We are not trying to suggest that the full domestic burden or indeed the enlarged domestic role affected only wives; what we do wish to stress is that the home may not function as a harmonious domestic unit with all parties acting in each other's interests or bearing equal domestic responsibility.

It seems probable that much of the conflict and tension experienced within the households of unemployed men is partly to do with the great difficulty of managing the home on a low income; but it also seems to arise from changed but largely unspoken expectations associated with the loss of the male breadwinner's 'provider' role. In terms of the traditional pattern for the division of domestic labour, this role legitimates low male participation in domestic work, and so the termination of male employment should, in equity, lead to a more egalitarian distribution of domestic work. However, because becoming unemployed is widely seen as a major threat to a man's identity and self-confidence, it could be interpreted as a further blow to his self-esteem to expect greater participation in what had hitherto been defined as 'women's work' (Green *et al.*, 1987b, pp. 53–4).

Morris's studies of redundant steelworkers and their wives in South Wales (1984, 1985) focus on the impact of male unemployment on patterns of domestic organisation, including financial arrangements, and local social networks. She studied husbands' readiness to assume tasks within the home which are culturally defined as 'women's work', and the extent to which their attitudes may be reinforced by membership of a predominantly male social network. The extent of any redistribution of domestic labour after redundancy was least where husbands had 'collective' social networks of this kind. Their social interactions typically took place with a stable single-sex group of others, occurring regularly on the same nights each week, within the same institutional setting. This lifestyle offers maximum scope for all-male groups of peers to exert pressure on members to conform to group norms, and in the context of reassessment of one's identity and expectations following redundancy, it is not difficult to visualise the effect on individual men of bar-room banter about the renegotiation of domestic responsibilities. Morris found that three-fifths of the male respondents with this 'collective' type of social network identified domestic tasks that they would not consider doing, compared with only a third of the other men. She also points out that the social activities of this group of men are highly predictable, as is the amount of personal spending money they require.

We have seen how male unemployment is typically associated with decreased household income; that the unaccustomed presence of a male partner in the home may disrupt customary household routines and leisure opportunities for women, as well as generating additional domestic work; and that the flexibility to respond positively to these changed conditions is reduced by community supports for a traditional, unequal domestic division of labour. Not surprisingly, many wives of unemployed men report feelings of stress and emotional strain (McKee and Bell, 1983, 1986), and over two-fifths of the wives in one study reported a deterioration in their marital relationship associated with their partner's unemployment (Burgoyne, 1985). The shortage of money and time for women's own leisure, in addition to the added burden of 'managing' the emotional strains of a partner's unemployment, make leisure opportunities outside the home a rare and prized commodity. Morris (1984, p. 507) identifies the practice of 'hobbling' as one popular response to these privations among the resourceful wives of redundant Welsh steelworkers: they combine sociability with small-scale income generation, by means of running 'clubs' (where goods are sold from a catalogue, and small weekly payments collected by the 'agent') and 'selling parties'.

Homeworking

Any contemporary analysis of the implications for women's leisure of changes in various kinds of working patterns – whether their own or that their male partner – needs to address the issue of homeworking. International shifts in labour market structures associated with the world recession of the late 1970s and early 1980s have dramatically altered patterns of employment. In many Western countries a decline in full-time male employment has been associated with an increase in part-time work, especially in the service industries, with many of these jobs being done by women. The proportion of the labour force in self-employment has increased (although the economic failure rates of newly established small businesses are high), as has homeworking (see Beechey, 1987; Allen and Wolkowitz, 1987; Green, Woodward and Hebron, 1988). In Britain the projected loss of full-time jobs (2.5 million between 1971 and 1990) is balanced by an increase in part-time work; one in five workers were employed part-time in 1980, with an estimated increase to one in four by the end of the decade (Beechey, 1987). Associated increases in the level of self-employment also have implications for a change in lifestyles, especially since much of that increase has occurred in the areas of casual work and subcontract-ing. Whilst it is true that some of the new self-employed are highly paid 'freelance' professionals in areas like computing, a larger group are low-paid workers on temporary and fixed-term contracts.

There is an important gender dimension to these changes: the decline in full-time work has disproportionately affected men, whereas the continuing expansion in part-time work can be largely accounted for by the increased participation of women in the labour force. The explanation is partly to do with the post-war demand for female part-time labour from employers seeking married women as a preferred labour force, because of the lower wages and employer's costs involved, together with an avoidance of the employment safeguards imposed by the Employment Protection Act. More recently there is an increased 'need' for job flexibility on the part of employers, the repercussions of which could mean not only changes in the length of work but also the conditions under which it is performed.

Debates about the future of work range from optimistic accounts which assume that the restructuring of employment brings with it higher levels of autonomy and job flexibility of benefit to the mass of workers (Clutterbuck and Hill, 1981; Handy, 1984) – and, of course, to employers – to more cautious analyses which document the disadvantages (Atkinson, 1984). The implications of such restructuring for equal opportunities in the labour market is a strong selling point utilised by management representatives of firms eager to 'flex' their workforce (that is, to put them onto new 'flexible' work patterns). The superficial nature of these arguments stands revealed, however, when the term 'manpower' is used to encompass female labour as well. Some of these firms (such as Rank Xerox) have begun to encourage their professional staff to work at home, partly on the advice of management consultants convinced by the advantages of professional networking; but the equal opportunities argument wears thin when one remembers the falling levels of an already small minority of professional women in, for example, the area of new technology. At an international conference on women and new technology held in Scotland in 1988, a management consultant to Rank Xerox espoused the virtues of homeworking for professional staff attempting to 'reconcile work and home, career and family', but the picture he painted of the worker using a home-based electronic office to network between Britain and California, 'more easily over a twenty four hour period', was starkly at odds with the research evidence on the realities of homeworking mainly carried out by women (Cragg and Dawson, 1981; Allen and Wolkowitz, 1987). One was left in little doubt about who was putting the children to bed and cooking the meal while this international exchange was occurring.

The advantages to employers of flexibility in the form of homeworking, such as reduction in overheads, the implementation of piece-work payments, and a reduction in their obligations to employees, far outweigh those experienced by the majority of workers on the receiving end.

Homeworking (paid work performed in the home), also known as outwork, is usually done in return for piece-work payment and is an international phenomenon. The vast majority of such work is done by women. Despite the widespread nature of homeworking and the vast differences in the goods produced, depending upon the geographical location of the worker, it remains a largely under-researched area. The upsurge of feminist research on women workers in the 1970s led to increased attention being paid to homeworkers, particularly in relation to the debate about the relationship between waged and unwaged forms of women's work and the concern over wage levels (Brown, 1974). But it was not until the 1980s, when homeworking appeared as part of the wider process of labour market restructuring, that it began to feature as a flexible option in management packages designed to combat problems ranging from reducing overheads and labour costs (Atkinson, 1984) to enhancing the quality of life. The study by Allen and Wolkowitz is highly critical of the idea of homeworking as a flexible option. They argue:

> Homeworking is characterised not only by its location in the home but by the conditions of employment . . . It is one of several types of employment in which the workforce is effectively casualised. (1987, p 5)

For Allen and Wolkowitz one of the effects of the process of casualisation is to turn certain categories of permanent members of the labour force into temporary workers to whom employers have few legal obligations. In this case the flexibility offered to employees by homeworking is far outweighed by the disadvantages of joining the ranks of low-paid, low-status, largely invisible workers with few employment protection rights.

The attractions of homeworking offered to highly paid professionals, such as the autonomy to decide when to work and the freedom to work at one's own pace, are illusory ideals for the bulk of homeworkers, whose hours and levels of work are largely determined by piece-work rates under the control of suppliers (Brown, 1974; Cragg and Dawson, 1981; Crine, 1979). Meeting production targets then becomes the responsibility of the home-worker; this appears to offer flexibility and choice, but in practice the workload is set by suppliers, many of whom utilise informal sanctions to persuade women to meet production targets – for example the mobilisation of kinship ties between supplier and worker (Allen and Wolkowitz, 1987). Far from enjoying a day characterised by odd moments of work interspersed with periods of leisure, the majority of women in Allen and Wolkowitz's study, based in West Yorkshire,

> did homework for 11 to 30 hours a week and twelve worked over 40 hours a week. Over a third worked in the evenings, as well as during the day and nearly as many worked at the weekend.

In a number of ways homeworking, far from enhancing the quality of working life, can, partly because of the lack of separation between paid and unpaid work, become a treadmill from which there is no escape.

We have already seen that both paid work performed outside the home and unpaid domestic work considerably constrain women's access to leisure time. Homeworking tends to combine the worst aspects of both activities, in terms of its implications for women's leisure. We have argued extensively elsewhere (Green and Hebron, 1988) that women's entitlement to leisure is highly dependent upon a number of variables, including their own and their male partner's perceptions of their having 'earned' the right to time off via paid work and the satisfactory fulfilment of maternal and partnership roles. Women engaged in paid work in the home are more likely to be subject to the control of male partners over their conditions and rates of work than those who work outside the home. Ironically it is usually family obligations, particularly childcare, that lead women to 'choose' homeworking in the first place, but the lack of independence associated with it can lead to an intensification of the traditional sexual division of labour which severely limits the potential autonomy and freedom involved.

We have already examined and rejected the common assertion that male partners are undertaking a more equal share of the domestic labour and childcare within the home, as the proportion of married women in employment increases. Where one or both partners are also engaged in *paid* work from home, women's responsibilities actually increase (Finch, 1983; Kirkham, 1987; Allen and Wolkowitz, 1987; Green, Hebron and Woodward, 1987b).

Family expectations in general, and husbands' attitudes in particular, are crucial for the definition and enforcement of the sexual division of labour. Many husbands prefer women to do paid work from home for a variety of reasons ranging from their being available full-time for children, to male unease about their female partner's independence in an external workplace. However, conflict may arise when women's paid work at home limits their time for unpaid work and family-based activities (Allen and Wolkowitz, 1987). Negotiations over women's access to independent leisure usually hinge on the couple's norms about responsibilities for childcare and each partner's entitlement to leisure (Green, Hebron and Woodward, 1987a), and may well become more heated if the pressures of homeworking are added to other sources of friction. A major issue concerns women's availability for spending time with male partners and children, and the quantity of such time is likely to be markedly reduced by paid work in the home. Allen and Wolkowitz (p. 177) state: 'Working at home leads as often to anger, tension and conflict as to co-operation and mutual aid'.

Likewise in households where the man is working from home, for example in a 'family' business, the use of the woman's time and energies for unpaid servicing roles can cause considerable resentment. This may be hard for the women concerned to challenge, given that it is legitimated by social expectations about a wife's role. Added to constraints on the wife's time are restrictions on living space, and availability of time and space for leisure. As Kirkham (1987, p. 8) comments in her study of the role of wives in small businesses, 'Garages are turned into workshops, the spare bedroom becomes an office and stock is kept in every available space'. Opportunities for women's home-based leisure are severely limited in this situation, as are their chances for leisure outside the home, by their assumption of the unpaid roles of secretary or salesperson. More important, the meaning of work in the domestic sphere has a gendered dimension. Men engaged in paid work from home (especially if part-time) can experience a sense of release from their traditional workplace, the office or factory; for women the home *is* their environment, whether that work is paid or unpaid. The absence of physical or temporal separation between paid and unpaid work, and the stress of unchanged high standards of housework and homemaking have clear implications for the availability of women's leisure-time, which is already mortgaged to the demands of others.

Conclusion

This assertion about the implications for women's leisure of having a male partner working from home echoes points made throughout this chapter about the lack of a clear distinction between the social worlds of home and work for many women. The cumulative weight of constraints on women's scope for autonomous leisure may be greater or less for varying groups of women: young, single women may have ample time and income available for enjoying their free time, their primary constraint being the social control mechanisms associated with patriarchal ideologies, as the next chapter examines. Older women who are housewives and mothers, particularly those from social backgrounds characterised by strongly held norms about female propriety, and those from low-income households, face a much greater struggle to achieve independent leisure. Running through the discussion in this chapter of the leisure opportunities available to women in a diversity of personal situations is a series of common issues.

First, any satisfactory analysis of the relationship between 'work' and 'leisure' for women needs to take a very broad view of what 'work' is, and not to confine its definition to paid employment. Second, it is vital to adopt a broad, holistic perspective in order to understand the complex interplay of cross-cutting influences between women's identities and obligations within the home and in the sphere of paid work. Traditional assumptions about orientations to employment based on male norms need to be reviewed for women in relation to other extra-work sets of commitments and roles. Third, women's employment, like women's leisure, often takes place within a contextual juggling act of balancing competing demands on their time, within a framework of ideologies where women's perceived entitlement to paid employment or to personal leisure may be highly problematic.

What does the future hold? Many of the changes resulting from the current restructuring of the labour market in Britain and other Western societies have major implications for the nature and extent of women's leisure. Alterations in employment patterns such as increasingly irregular hours, employment periods, contracts and working conditions, take place within a patriarchal society characterised by class divisions, and are more likely to benefit white, middle-class men with professional careers. Although, in theory, the promise of more flexible working practices could lead to a better quality of life for all workers, in reality the benefits or privations will be mediated by divisions of class, gender and race.

In the face of a persistently unequal sexual division of labour in the home and a reinforcement of images of 'normal' family life as peopled by 'caring' wives and mothers and 'dependable, hard earning' husbands and fathers, real opportunities for change will involve protracted struggle and negotiation. Far from releasing women for more flexible access to leisure, increased pressures to take on part-time employment (whether in the workplace or the home) may actually reduce their already limited opportunities for leisure. Likewise, earlier male retirement, high levels of unemployment (whether for women, male partners or adult children) and increased rates of male self-employment and home-based work are all likely to erode women's scope for autonomous leisure by increasing the demands made on them as wives, mothers and housewives.

6

The process of social control in public and private spheres

Introduction

We have argued earlier that women share a subordinate social position which is mediated by divisions of social class and race, as well as by divisions of age and marital status. It is important to analyse the components of the process of social control which maintain that subordination. Gender is clearly a key dimension in understanding the form and content of leisure in capitalist society, and the specific experiences of individuals in relation to leisure activities and attitudes in the 'public' and 'private' spheres. At the level of ideology, sexuality is a central factor in representations of women both pursuing their own leisure interests and servicing the leisure of others. Sexuality is also a crucial element in representations of appropriate ways for women and men to spend time, which assumes particular significance in an examination of pub cultures and drinking behaviour.

Leisure, gender and associated representations of sexuality

Leisure in contemporary society is now 'big business' as a sector of employment, and as an industry manufacturing and marketing leisure goods and providing services. We are offered an increasingly diverse selection of 'choices' in ways to spend our leisure, from home-based activities such as the use of videos and exercise equipment, to organised leisure in the form of sports or nightclubs. A major trend in recent years has been towards home-based leisure activities, with a focus on family entertainment (*Social Trends*, 1982). This is often represented in images which observe the fact that the vast majority of leisure activities at home and in the public sphere are subject to gender divisions. Even if men and women are engaged in the same activity, be it watching television, reading or listening to music, the form assumed by the activity is often gender-differentiated.

Leisure industries commonly use advertisements which feature women as servicing agents of leisure, whether in the role of employee behind the bar of a public house or counter of a fast-food restaurant, or the role of wife and mother serving snacks to husband and children while they watch television. Even a superficial analysis of such images reveals that servicing other people's leisure involves work for women. Less obvious is the form taken by such images of women, especially those used in advertising. Popular images, when decoded, reveal particular representations of class and race as well as gender, and frequently contain an age dimension too. Leisure images reflect social divisions which are ultimately rooted in the fundamental structures of capitalism, and particular sets of leisure activities help to realise those social divisions by giving them expression and legitimation.

In the area of gender divisions, popular leisure images contribute to the reproduction of ideologies of masculinity and femininity via the accompanying representations of appropriate roles and activities. A major ingredient of these images is sexuality, packaged in such a way as to convey excitement, romance and perhaps danger. Sexual images of women are used to sell commercial products ranging from cars to cooking utensils, and usually convey messages which reinforce the traditional roles of women and men. Feminist analyses of advertising have revealed the complexity of the representations of gender involved, and have examined the target audience (Winship, 1981). The sexual woman is signified by fragmented bodily parts, most frequently hair, eyes, legs and hips. It is not usually necessary to resort to images of breasts and buttocks when a brief glimpse of a silk-encased knee will convey the message as clearly and more subtly. Goffman (1979, p. 7) states that: 'feminity and masculinity are in a sense prototypes of essential expression – something that can be conveyed fleetingly in any social situation'. Such fleeting images are commonly used to advertise leisure, whether it be products, facilities or the 'leisure experience' itself. Along with the exercise bike, jogging suit or alcoholic drink, the consumer is buying sex, which is seen as adding excitement and glamour to what might at best be a mundane activity. The basic ingredients of the actual leisure experience, such as physical exercise, and the attendant alterations in bodily functions are, however, minimised, as the following example illustrates. Adverts for sanitary towels, products intimately associated with the most powerful expression of female sexuality, the menstrual cycle, mask the force of this image. 'The bleeding' which signifies fertility and reproduction is represented as just another 'understain' to be deodorised and hidden from public view. Those adverts which seek to sell such products through images of women supposedly engaging in sport are particularly interesting in this context. They encourage us (women) to buy the product, apparently as an aid to facilitating our engagement in such activities, whilst also conveying the Western taboo on displaying the physical signs of it such as sweat and blood. Sexuality is still the key focus here, but in a deodorised, highly packaged form.

The key point of interest in the above discussion lies in the contradiction between, on the one hand, the ways in which women's bodies are used in advertisements to represent pleasure and sexuality as freely available ingredients of the leisure available for consumption, and, on the other hand, the fact that the behaviour of real women entering such venues is subject to close surveillance by both individual men and groups of men. Expressions of sexuality, whether in the form of dress or behaviour, are seen as contravening the limits of respectability and draw sanctions ranging from unwanted attention or social disapproval to overt male hostility (Green, Hebron and Woodward, 1987c).

Ideologies of respectability

The concept of respectability constitutes a key element in the construction and representation of women. As discussed in Chapter 2, ideologies construct specific aspects of the social world as 'natural' and 'universal'. Ideologies of masculinity and femininity are a vital component of the commonsense knowledge on which we draw to make sense of our experience and to inform our behaviour; cultural stereotypes form an integral part of such ideologies. However, the cultural representation of gender comprises more than simply images of women (Pollock, 1977). It is linked to a broader system of signification and to real relations which are historically constituted. The categories of masculinity and femininity, which form an essential part of the process through which gender ideologies are produced, are both constructed in relation to specific historical conditions and exist today in systematic and even predictable terms (Barrett, 1980). Winship (1983, p. 35) discusses the fact that ideologies 'offer only a partial or selective, and sometimes contradictory knowledge and explanation'. They are social constructions closely tied in with the interests of dominant social groups, which in this case are patriarchal and sited within capitalist social relations. As we argued in Chapter 2, ideological stereotypes of women in contemporary capitalism divide them into those respectable women who are or will be wives, mothers and daughters, and women who are beyond the limits of respectability as whores or 'fallen women'. This dual classification ties the majority of women into a particular stereotype in relation to the family and prescribes for women the roles of housewife and mother. All women are considered to be either potential mothers and housewives or sex objects; class and racial differences are rendered invisible, except in relation to the supposed deviant minority who are represented within parallel stereotypes – for example the devoted mammy, and the exotic black seductress (Bryan, Dadzie and Scafe, 1985). Empirical studies carried out by Hobson (1981) and Westwood (1984) emphasise the extent to which courtship and the early stages of marriage and motherhood limit acceptable behaviour for women, and leisure activities in particular, to only those which are deemed appropriate and respectable for married women. During the phase of 'serious courting' the vast majority of women give up their own spare-time pleasures in favour of the joint activities linked with 'going steady' and 'saving to get married'. Relationships with friends independent of the couple, particularly girlfriends, are discontinued, often to be regretted at a later stage when loneliness and isolation ensue.

Our own data illustrate this clearly, particularly in the case of women with young children who have given up paid work and may have moved away from their families:

> You don't meet anybody, you know, there's nobody round here who I know really well, only next door and she's got her own shop so she's working. (Green, Hebron and Woodward, 1987b, p. 155)

Westwood's study vividly illustrates the overwhelming desire shared by young working-class women for romance and marriage as an escape from the drudgery of low-paid, unskilled work on a factory floor. Having longed for the 'liberation' of their own home and family, the majority of these women experienced heavy disillusionment when they discovered themselves to be caught in the trap of 'the budgie cage' of married life.

Wives and mothers

This feeling of being trapped occurred for many women even before they had children, and was related to feelings of powerlessness in relationships with partners and the tiredness associated with the burden of unpaid domestic work which they were expected to assume in addition to any paid work. A consistent finding in both the two studies cited above and in our own, concerns the heavy emphasis on cleanliness and order in working-class domestic life. The women interviewed never had sufficient time to clean and polish to the standard which they considered desirable. This order and cleanliness is tied to respectability and the 'proper' fulfilment of the wife/mother role. The condition of the house is one of the few tangible examples of the physical manifestation of those roles, which makes it a source of continuing anxiety for women who feel they lack the time and energy to maintain it to an acceptable level. The experience and advice of older women on the sheer drudgery of such tasks is belied by their own position as mothers and wives. As Westwood (1984, p. 170) notes,

> Housework, family work, domestic labour, whatever it is to be called, is surrounded by a powerful mystique which each generation of wives creates anew, making it their own.

Social control and everyday life

This mystique surrounding women's domestic role is reinforced by prevailing norms about respectable female behaviour. Images of the 'normal woman' are contained in the stereotypes which form a major part of ideologies of femininity and are built into both the formation and implementation of social policy and into everyday relations between individuals (Hutter and Williams, 1981). It is only when we examine the content of such stereotypes, in addition to the parallel stereotypes of so-called deviant women, that the extent and nature of the control involved is revealed. Although many of the beliefs and norms relating to women's behaviour are embodied in external forms such as social policy, legislation and hierarchy, many are also internalised as part of the fabric of everyday life and cease to be visible as value systems or one set of culturally formed beliefs. It can also be argued that the less clearly particular norms are articulated, the harder it is, first, to identify them as such, and, second, to challenge them. As Smart and Smart (1978) note, it is all too easy to see covert forms of oppression as part of the individual psychologies of oppressed women, rather than locating them in the public sphere as part of internalised ideological structures.

One of the major factors which ties women to the home and limits their access to the public sphere is their position as mothers. As argued above, the stereotype of the mother provides the key to understanding the relative immobility of the majority of women so designated. Perkins' (1979) analysis of stereotypes highlights the source of their strength as based upon three factors: their simplicity, their immediate recognisability, and their implicit reference to an assumed consensus of beliefs. The third factor is particularly apt in relation to an analysis of the stereotype of the 'good mother', a figure who occupies a dominant position in representations of women. The main ingredient involves the notion of sacrifice (Seiter, 1986). Mothers are first and foremost emotionally and physically accessible to all family members at all times. According to Seiter, the stereotype of the 'good mother' represents her as born with a particular set of 'natural' characteristics which fit her for such a role. This obscures the fact that motherhood is a learned role, acquired in the nuclear family as a result of the sexual division of labour, and is subject to historical and cultural variations.

The linked stereotype of the 'good wife' is constituted by similar characteristics (self-sacrifice, obedience and cleanliness), as is shown in the discussion of Westwood's and Hobson's work. In fact these characteristics, as Seiter (1986, p. 67) argues, have little to do with the strict requirements of childcare, but are essential to

> a social order in which women serve men, care for their material needs (the reproductive work of shopping, cooking, cleaning etc.) as well as their emotional ones, and in which women are heterosexual, mono- gamous and sexually available to the men they care for.

The above characteristics fit the wife of a traditional marriage where the women has very little social power. This notion of sacrifice and unending accessibility to others is consented to by other women (such as mothers and sisters) and is passed on to daughters together with the necessary copying strategies.

Paradoxically the very support networks offered by women to other women, although frequently positive and benign, are often fraught with contradictions in that they can function to reinforce patriarchal power and limit the possibility of challenges to it. Guilt is probably one of the most powerful factors that ties women to their children in the home – a socially induced guilt which illustrates the implicit assumption that a mother's place is in the home with her child. Correlated with this is the deep-seated belief that young children should not be left with strangers, a norm captured in the following comment from one of the women in our study who had a child of three and was pregnant again:

> I wouldn't really have left him with anybody for a full day. My mum has him for the afternoon you know. But I wouldn't really leave him with anyone but my husband for a full day unless it was an exception. (Green, Hebron and Woodward, 1987b, p. 74)

The traditional domestic division of labour and the care of children have direct consequences for women's access to leisure. It can severely restrict the time available for leisure, particularly when women are engaged in paid work as well, in a way that is not true for men. In contrast, the majority of men's non-work time is potentially available for leisure. For women, domestic obligations are not neatly confined to eight-hour slots or clearly demarcated from leisure. It is not simply the amount of time that is a problem; it is also the quality of the time that is available. As Wimbush (1986,

p. 60) comments in her study of leisure in the lives of mothers with pre-school-age children:

> Being a mother had made it more difficult to put their own personal interests first without feeling guilty. So, leisure increasingly became something derived from, or enjoyed in conjunction with, obligations and duties to the home and family.

Even so-called free time may be interrupted by the demands of other household members, given that wives and mothers are almost always 'on call'. Women's major responsibility for the home and family also means that when they do have some time for leisure, they may be too tired to do anything except sit down and relax.

Alcohol, drinking and the limits of 'decent' behaviour

Although, as we argue in Chapter 1, leisure is a difficult concept to define, seemingly vague and amorphous in terms of its content and boundaries, 'time free from constraints' emerges as a central component in responses from women in our own and parallel studies of women and leisure (Wimbush, 1986; Deem, 1986a). The concepts of relaxation and sociability are clearly perceived to be important, and it seems that for many women, having fun or 'a laugh' in the company of others, outside the home, constitutes 'real leisure'. However, this is one area which frequently becomes a source of conflict with male partners. In the Sheffield-based survey, 11 per cent of the women with partners stated that they would like to go out more often with their partners, but reported that the latter were unwilling to do this, many preferring to spend their evenings in the home:

> I used to want to go out because I do like socialising. My husband used to work outside and when he came home all he wanted was his armchair and the television. (Green, Hebron and Woodward, 1987b, p. 82)

For most women who live in a family situation with male partners, couple-based leisure seems to be the ideal, reflecting dominant ideologies of romantic love and togetherness. Despite such images, it is common for both men and women to engage in independent leisure outside the home with members of the same sex. Men are more likely than women to continue patterns of independent leisure established while they are single, whereas married women tend to sacrifice such pursuits, particularly when they become mothers. Visits to the pub with 'the lads' are a frequent and accepted leisure activity for men, despite the objections of female partners. In contrast, the issue of women's independent leisure generates a great deal of conflict, the level varying in relation to the type of activities involved. Traditionally female activities that accord with ideologies of femininity (such as aerobics, keep fit, flower arranging and coffee mornings) are approved of and deemed acceptable; others, such as a night out on the town visiting pubs or discos unaccompanied by male partners, are not (Deem, 1986a; Green, Hebron and Woodward, 1987b). Many of the couples interviewed in the Sheffield study had reached a consensus whereby women's occasional nights out with female friends were accepted, with the proviso that they should not become too regular. This was particularly the case for mothers of young children.

Unless couples have maintained patterns of separate activities from an early stage in their relationship, it might be difficult to negotiate independent pursuits. It can be seen as threatening for a partner to begin to seek personal leisure outside the home. Leisure is a sphere where sexuality has a high profile, particularly in commercial venues where alcohol is served such as pubs and nightclubs. Attempts by women to frequent such places without male partners are often seen as signals of dissatisfaction with current relationships, and may signify the search for a new partner (Burgoyne and Clark, 1984). Age and social class divisions are important here, particularly with reference to male jealousy. Class differences seem to affect the form of male resistance to wives' or partners' independent leisure, rather than the level of it. A middle-class husband in the Sheffield study commented that more frequent evenings out by his wife might be an indicator of marital dissatisfaction:

I perhaps would not be unduly concerned about it, although if there was a tendency for it to be . . . I wouldn't want to say 'Well you can't do that' or 'you shouldn't be doing that', but I would say 'well', you know, 'is there anything happening in our relationship', look at it that way 'which has occasioned it, perhaps' and that's the only reason I would see her doing that. (Green, Hebron and Woodward, 1987b, p. 209)

In contrast a working-class husband, unemployed at the time of the survey, operated more overtly to constrain his wife's independent leisure activities. The woman preferred to go out on her own because she found joint leisure, tailored to his requirements, boring:

> well, if she wants to spend the same as me, she can go out every night with me if she wants, you know, I've no objection to that at all . . . I'd rather her go out with me and go to one of the places I like to go than her stop in. You know, I get a bit annoyed sometimes, if she won't come out and do things I want to do. (Green, Hebron and Woodward, 1987a, p. 116)

As for the other unemployed families in the study, money for leisure for this couple was very limited, the husband having the major share of it. If his wife insisted on having independent activities rather than sharing his, he made life difficult by refusing money and co-operation, including childcare. Level of income was one of the clearest issues tied to social class which highlighted differences in male strategies of control over women's time and leisure. In the middle-class households, although women theoretically had access to joint funds and resources for independent leisure, they rarely exercised their right to it, partly because of the unspoken agreement that joint leisure or being with the family was preferable. Working-class women also operated within this ideological climate, but suffered from the additional disadvantage of having to negotiate with partners for a share of scarce joint resources.

It is clear that women do share some common experiences as a consequence of their gender and that their leisure is controlled and constructed into what are perceived as acceptable forms. This process of social control operates in a non-uniform but consistent way across class and age differences and is most visible when women attempt to contravene the limits of 'respectable' behaviour.

'Ladies in the lounge bar only': men's control over public places

Associations between female sexuality, the pursuit of leisure and pleasure, and public houses has a long history. This has been represented in a variety of media images, the variations often signifying major changes in social attitudes towards drinking. While women's bodies are routinely used in the advertising designed to sell alcohol, ranging from beer to the most exotic new cocktail, women as consumers of these products are deemed more socially acceptable in the home than as regulars at the local pub.

As Hey (1986) notes, throughout history the pub has been a male preserve, with women being treated as 'guests' in a domain which is both a public space and at the same time a male arena. In Victorian times, though, it was usual for working-class women to frequent both the rural ale house and the urban pub (Hunt and Satterlee, 1987). The typical customer at the former was, however, male, and the patterns of female visits were as much regulated by social convention as they are today. Women visited ale houses accompanied by male partners or friends, and those who went alone were viewed at worst as promiscuous, and were potentially subject to assault, and the least sanction they could expect was unwanted attention from men. The situation was complicated by the fact that women worked in both pubs and ale houses. Available historical data indicate that concern for the morality of female drinkers and associated attempts to impose restrictions on their use of facilities were hampered by the fact that many women were involved in the commercial sale of alcohol, and 'victualising' was seen as a suitable occupation for widows in particular (Hunt and Satterlee, 1987). In addition, the link between male drinking and the use of the services of prostitutes in Victorian pubs rendered regular alcohol consumption in such places both non-respectable and morally suspect for all women. As Hey (1986, p. 33) states,

> In the popular imagination, drunkenness in women equated with sexually improper conduct in a way that rendered women who drank beneath contempt. Their lack of self-restraint was viewed as far more threatening and morally offensive than the equivalent male action.

Such contradictory attitudes, albeit in a different form, linger on today, surprisingly unchanged. The Victorian legacy of gin drinking among the so-called 'dangerous classes' concerned Victorian philanthropists who attempted to control such behaviour through legislation. Similar concerns are evident in contemporary social attitudes towards female drunkenness, especially among women who are mothers. As outlined above, stereotypes of mothers represent them as moral guardians, and the loss of control implied by drunkenness is seen as leading to behaviour that conflicts with the capacity to perform their primary roles. Drunkenness in men (linked with aggressive behaviour) may be tolerated as an acceptable aspect of masculinity, but it is deplored in women and associated with promiscuity, despite the fact that studies of women with alcohol-related problems have shown them to be no more or less promiscuous than other women (Otto, 1981).

There is evidence to suggest that female drinking patterns have changed significantly since the last war. Otto links such changes partly with the increase in middle-class women's employment in stressful jobs where there is a norm of heavy drinking. These changes are obviously also linked to the liberalisation of attitudes towards social drinking for women and men, both at home and in leisure venues. Despite a broader social acceptance of alcohol consumption, there is no sign of any corresponding liberalisation of attitudes towards female drunkenness. Women alcoholics are portrayed as either 'bad' or 'mad', with the response from relatives and practitioners tending towards assumptions which rely on depression or related psychiatric conditions as causal.

This brief summary of the legacy of Victorian pub cultures and changing social attitudes towards female drinking provides a framework for the discussion of current responses to women's consumption of alcohol in leisure venues.

Several studies of pub cultures and related social relations have focused on the function of such cultures in reinforcing ideologies of masculinity (Whitehead, 1976; Hunt and Satterlee, 1987). Social relations between men and women in the setting of the pub provide representations of 'normal' patriarchal beliefs and values. The teasing and banter engaged in by men (usually at the expense of, or in relation to, women) in leisure venues is generally regarded as 'good fun' and an acceptable display of masculinity, whereas if women attempt to reverse the situation by responding in kind, such behaviour is regarded as provocative and open to sanction. As Smart and Smart (1978) note, this form of informal group process is a major source of social control and can be specifically related to the control of sexuality. Both studies cited above take the form of case studies of women's use of rural pubs and the associated gender relations characteristic of village life. Although Whitehead's study (carried out in the late 1960s in Herefordshire) distinguishes between farmers' wives and non-farming wives, rather than using the more precise class distinctions employed in Hunt and Satterlee's 1980s study based in Melton, East Anglia, the men's use of techniques in the social control of women within the pub are remarkably consistent across the studies, despite differences of time and geographical location.

Women in these rural communities rarely enter the local pub on their own:

> women to a large extent entered the pub as appendages of men. They came into the pub as sisters, wives, daughters, nieces and girlfriends but hardly ever only as women. The single female drinker was still largely unacceptable. (Hunt and Satterlee, 1987, p. 17)

For the occasional all-female drinking session, the women in Whitehead's study sought pubs outside the parish boundaries, presumably to avoid social sanctions from local men. The only exception to this pattern of drinking occurs in the Melton study, in the case of the women's darts team at one of the three pubs involved. The team was composed of working-class women and gave local women a chance both to 'get out of the house' and to occupy space in the pub in their own right. However, they were still constrained by lack of access to transport and childcare, paid work and kinship obligations, and by the constant vigilance of male drinkers intent on maintaining their patriarchal control over the pub arena. The techniques used to sustain this control range from hostile silence and avoidance, to verbal abuse and ridicule, and are an example of a consistent set of patriarchal controls routinely used by men to control women's behaviour in public places.

Class is an important factor in an analysis of both the pattern of women's drinking, and of the attitudes and responses of significant males. Hunt and Satterlee's evidence suggests that middle-class women are freer to engage in drinking sessions at the pub, due to their ownership of and access to private transport, independent incomes and, perhaps most significantly in the case of the Melton women, few kinship ties in the village. However, they still mainly visited the pub with male escorts and rarely bought a round when in a group of mixed friends, which served to marginalise them as regulars. These relatively subtle ways of keeping women in their place contrast with the more colourful exchanges reported in Whitehead's work, which appear more overtly related to the reinforcement of masculinity. Rumour of women's supposed infidelity, together with deliberate verbal abuse, usually in the form of suggestive jokes, combined both to control the women in the pub and to re-affirm male group cohesion. The joking or teasing elements of male humour, particularly when related to sexual prowess, is contradictory in that it demonstrates both bonding and rivalry between men. At another level it also reinforces the implicit assumption that women are property in need of male protection – a process that is subject to a complex system of rights and duties closely connected with family and kinship ties and obligations. The unreasonable nature of male dominance becomes obscured in the representation of male jealousy as a 'normal' response to wives and female kin members being exposed to the attentions of other men.

One of the few sources or resistance to this power balance that was open to the women concerned, involved building female solidarity as a basis from which to confront the men. However, as Whitehead (1976) and Hey (1986) both note, men are hostile to such solidarity and go to great lengths to subvert it. This finding is supported by the Sheffield study, in which the majority of couples interviewed confirmed the view that men were threatened by 'women's nights out', which they perceived as providing opportunities for women's contact and liaisons with other men. Whitehead makes the additional point that all-women social networks can represent a threat to male dominance through wives' transmission of personal details about men to each other which transgress the private boundaries of coupledom.

An interesting point that emerges from all the studies discussed above concerns the paucity of occasions when women do actually manage to engage in independent leisure. When questioned closely about such occasions, couples in the Sheffield study admitted that these were mostly rare events despite the amount of male disapproval reported. An additional factor in explaining the infrequency of such outings is related to most women's limited access to private transport and their fear of being out alone after dark. In the survey, 53 per cent said that fear of walking alone after dark limited their choice of activities (Green, Hebron and Woodward, 1987b). Existing studies of male violence against women (Dobash and Dobash, 1980; Hanmer and Saunders, 1984; Stanko, 1985) stress the fact that this fear is both widespread among women and justified:

> Being on guard for women, though, is not paranoia, it is reasonable caution. Many women have encountered men's threatening, intimidating or violent behaviour at first hand. (Stanko, 1985, p. 2)

The experience of public violence and the fear of violence from strangers in public places has a definite effect on women's sense and use of freedom, leading them to restrict their movements. Hanmer and Saunders (1983) state that this fear of public abuse is fed by the media, informal rumour and the shared personal experiences of women. Their pilot study of violence in Leeds found that since the five-year period during which the 'Yorkshire Ripper' murders took place, the majority of women had substantially restricted their movements. This included never walking alone at night and using private and public transport much more frequently.

Such 'avoidance' strategies also led to a greater reliance on male partners and friends for protection, and a heightened awareness by women of their own behaviour and alleged potential culpability in provoking violence. The extreme end of this continuum of representations of female responsibility is manifest in the following stereotype, which involves the portrayal of female alcoholics as sexually 'loose', blameworthy victims. Miller's (1986) US study of the experience of conflict and violence by alcoholic women stresses the fact that societal responses to the victim who has been drinking may be very different from the public response to 'respectable' non-drinking victims, a difference which may also have the effect of reducing the level of formal or informal intervention. Despite this, US statistics demonstrate that violent victimisation of women is not related to women's consumption of alcohol (Berk *et al.*, 1983), although the presence of an alcoholic male partner increases the level of 'spousal' violence directed at women. Such evidence underlines the contradictions involved in women turning to male partners for protection against public male violence, when they are in fact more likely to experience violence at the hands of men they know than from strangers (Radford, 1985). We are warned from childhood not to trust strangers, but as Stanko (1985, p. 9) wryly comments: 'somehow they forget to warn us about men we know: our fathers, our acquaintances, our co-workers, our lovers, our teachers'.

The apparently 'extreme' experiences of male violence discussed above, and the everyday fears of women seeking access to safe, independent leisure outside the home, are linked. Male violence against women is judged in relation to the degree of respectability demonstrated by individual women. This link is not only made by official agencies such as the police and judges, but is also frequently internalised by women themselves, particularly when seeking an explanation for male violence. As Edwards (1987, p. 161) observes:

> From cases of common assault to woundings to the ultimate of violence – homicide – the female victim in both theory and practice is frequently monitored for the extent to which she provoked her own demise. The concept of provocation, although not a defence, can be taken into consideration when deciding sentence in common assault, assault occasioning actual bodily harm and grievous bodily harm.

Leisure for women of all social classes is highly constrained by dominant assumptions about what constitutes respectable 'womanly' behaviour, and is constantly overshadowed by the values of a society with a large investment in maintaining 'stable' family units. Once identified as primarily wives, mothers and daughters, women's sexual identities must be hidden or 'packaged' in an acceptable non-threatening form. In fact, far from being a freely flowing, rampant force which – if left unfettered – could constitute a threat to moral standards, sexuality is shaped by social forces and, as Weeks (1986, p. 25) argues, is extremely susceptible to organisation and regulation: 'Sexuality is not given, it is a product of negotiation, struggle and human agency'.

Freedom to work but not to play: acceptable leisure

Although the popular view is that men and women in contemporary society enjoy equality of leisure opportunity, women's leisure is interwoven with other aspects of their lives, in contrast to the 'chunks' of time that most men are able to devote to their leisure. Women's leisure choices are effectively narrowed to the range of pursuits and venues deemed acceptable and appropriate. This narrowing can be observed in the leisure patterns of young women, which are substantially affected by the appearance of a 'steady' boyfriend (Griffin, 1981; McCabe, 1981). Many young women tend to drop their own leisure pursuits in favour of couple-based activities, unlike young men, who continue to meet 'the lads' on a regular basis. However, this is not always the case; some studies report Friday night as 'lasses' nights' (Westwood, 1984; Beuret and Makings, 1987; Griffiths, 1988) when groups of young women 'hit the town' together, reserving Saturday nights for their boyfriends.

What is clear is that maintaining female friendships involves complicated planning, and time spent with girlfriends is usually fitted around couple-based leisure. This is partly a response to the effects of dominant ideologies of romantic love which highlight the couple relationship as the ideal, and partly a preparation for what many women perceive as the 'real world' of marriage and motherhood:

> I tended to cut everyone else off, you see, and just sort of be with him all the time, so yes, I mean sports just stopped, I don't play sports any more. (Green, Hebron and Woodward, 1987b, p. 48)

The process of socialisation into this state begins to operate early on in women's lives. Westwood's (1984) study of factory and family life documents the amount of time spent on romantic fantasies and marriage plans by young women bored with the tedium of factory routines. It is here that views are exchanged about the 'realities' of married life, gilded by the hopeful sparkle of engagement rings and joint savings for the marital home. The necessary effort of pooling incomes by engaged couples, however, led to more than a financial investment in married life. Social life became rationed and routinised, which led to disillusionment for some of the women, while others were prepared to sacrifice autonomy for what they perceived as access to the resources controlled by men. Despite this,

> saving together did not necessarily mean suffering together. It seemed that the men had fewer restrictions on them. They still bought motor bikes and went to the pub for a night out with the blokes while Angie or Beth stayed home to do the ironing. (Westwood, p. 110)

As Hobson's (1981) work and the Sheffield study confirm, not only do young women tend to give up both their spare-time activities and their girlfriends once they are 'going steady', but in addition, once the men are sure of their affections, they may refuse to go to dances or discos with the women. This pattern continues into married life, much to the regret of the now wives, many of whom gained considerable pleasure out of this leisure activity (Hobson, 1978; Deem, 1986a). As Hobson (1981, p. 109) observes, it is almost as if a home and family are goals for the young women alone, whilst

> Men seem to have 'gone along' with the idea of saving for marriage . . . However, it seems that the men still had their 'night out' with their mates or their visits to the local football matches.

There is ample evidence that women tend to gravitate towards conforming to traditional stereotypes of femininity and respectability once they begin seriously considering marriage, and part of this process involves engaging in 'acceptable' leisure pursuits. Once married with young children, the element of choice over leisure largely disappears, due to the constraints imposed by shortage of time and economic resources. All the young single women interviewed in the qualitative stage of the Sheffield study experienced their independence as a necessarily temporary phenomenon, closely linked to being single (Green and Hebron, 1988). This expectation is confirmed by the mothers of young children interviewed at the same stage, many of whom reported 'time to themselves' in the home as their major leisure activity. The mother of a four-and-a-half year old snatched the odd half-hour when her child was at school:

> Just when he's at school I try and get what I've got to do, but I always leave half an hour from the time I fetch him to do, even if its only going in the bath or washing your hair, little things like that, what you take for granted, because you can't do it because you can't leave him. (Green, Hebron and Woodward, 1987c, p. 159)

Male strategies of control

Even if women do not feel that their leisure choices become circumscribed by 'settling down' with a steady male partner, for many a decline in their circle of independent friends and the unwelcoming nature of many leisure venues serve to restrict effective choice. The attitudes of both individual men and groups of men are highly significant in this context.

Hey (1986, p. 6–7) provides apt illustration of this point in her semi-literary versions of her own experiences in pubs in the company of groups of women, where they were the subject of verbal abuse and ridiculing gestures from men within minutes of sitting down together. In a similar way women's attempts to have leisure independently of their partners can be a major source of conflict, particularly if it involves leaving the home. If men are not happy about their female partner's activities they can behave in a number of ways which are consistent with, and serve to reinforce, patriarchal norms. A common response reported in both the Sheffield study and Green and Parry's (1982) work involved sulking or 'having a face on' – silent disapproval which was difficult to challenge due to the deliberate refusal to make explicit the grounds for it. An alternative (and very common) strategy is to play on women's own guilt, a strategy that is justified and legitimated by the full weight of patriarchal ideologies of being a good wife and/or mother. If such forms of controlling behaviour do not dissuade their partners, men may explicitly exercise male authority by simply forbidding women to go. This may be reinforced by threatening or actual physical violence. The important point here is that violence against wives should not be viewed as isolated incidents but as part of the whole relationship between the couple. In a very detailed study of wife-beating carried out in Scotland, the Dobashes concluded that:

> The correct interpretation of violence between husbands and wives conceptualises such violence as the *extension* of the domination and control of husbands over wives. (Dobash and Dobash, 1980, p. 15, our emphasis)

The social control of public spaces

A significant aspect of the social control of women's leisure is the regulation of their access to public places, and their behaviour in such places. This is grounded in the question of women's right to occupy particular spaces. From the Victorian era, if not earlier, women's proper place has traditionally been seen as the home, with men monopolising the public sphere. For over a century women have been discouraged from having a high profile in many areas of public life (Hall, 1979). With regard to leisure, many venues are male-dominated, and women are either made unwelcome there or are only welcome on specific terms. Male social control of public spaces, including leisure venues, can take a number of forms, ranging from silent disapproval, joking or ridiculing behaviour, and sexual innuendo through to open hostility (Green, Hebron and Woodward, 1987c). Most women experience some discomfort if they go to pubs, clubs, restaurants or wine bars without a male escort, and unwanted attention from men is not uncommon. Eighty-four per cent of the Sheffield survey respondents reported feeling uncomfortable about going to a pub on their own, and 90 per cent were uncomfortable alone in wine bars, rising to 93 per cent feeling uncomfortable on their own in working men's clubs (Green, Hebron and Woodward, 1987b, Appendix 3). Such control can constrain women's behaviour even where they are part of a mixed gender group, and it serves to confirm their unequal status. Hunt and Satterlee (1987, p. 10) note that when a woman within a group at the Griffin Pub in Melton (the female researcher) attempted to buy a round,

> Her attempt was rejected by the men when one of them remarked 'ladies don't do that', at which point he promptly bought the round himself.

Ideologies about appropriate feminine behaviour reinforce the popular assumption that 'respectable' women have no place in such venues without a male escort. Unaccompanied single women or women in groups are therefore considered to be potentially sexually 'available'. While conducting research in Yorkshire, Middleton's presence in the bar of the sports and social club led to her either being reclassified as 'not there', or subjected to the sort of joking that defines her as an 'object to be screwed' (Imray and Middleton, 1983, p. 23).

Reinforcement of male attitudes and strategies

In the context of everyday life women make individual choices and enter into negotiations about appropriate ways to conduct themselves, with both male partners and female relatives and friends, which take place within a framework of constraints, both material and ideological. Women's subordinate social position is reinforced and maintained at one level by material inequalities and at another (though necessarily linked) by ideological processes. This process is ongoing, with the social control of women as one element within the struggle to maintain male hegemony which sets the limits of appropriate female behaviour. Without resorting to a crude conspiratorial model, it is possible to pin-point a number of ways in which women's lives are regulated on a day-to-day basis within the structures of patriarchal capitalism. We have argued that the framework within which individual women enter into negotiations over their access to leisure can be seen as a continuum of social control (Green, Hebron and Woodward, 1987c). At one end of this continuum are forms of behaviour which use physical violence to control women; at the other are non-coercive forms, or what could be termed control through 'consent'. It is to this 'soft and subtle' set of controls that we now turn.

Although the outcome of the social control process discussed above is the maintenance of patriarchal values and male hegemony, the process involved is not the simple 'policing' of one gender by another, but a complex process operating across a number of levels. Two key features worthy of mention are the 'strategies of avoidance' that women develop from an early age and the role of women themselves in restraining each other's behaviour.

Several studies of women in paid work have pointed to the ways in which women experience difficulty when confronted with what amount to male-dominated spheres of work, fed by informal masculine networks of control and expertise (Smith, 1976; Purcell, 1979; Pollert, 1981; Westwood, 1984). Women may be deliberately excluded from areas of knowledge and techniques which are crucial in gaining promotion, especially where informal networks are the main channel of communication. Although these networks have a crucial bearing upon what occurs in the workplace, they are often most visible and effective in leisure situations which involve groups of workers ostensibly taking time off. Smith's study of the gender relations among Fleet Street journalists in London points to the difficulty women had in gaining membership to informal groups where stories and newsworthy information were exchanged, a process which mostly occurred in pubs. In particular he comments that:

> the key learning areas remain strong male preserves, where the development of such sub-cultures is most facilitated, and this is the reason masculine supremacy is maintained. (Smith, 1976, p. 82)

Women who are successful in traditionally masculine fields frequently achieve such success by cutting themselves off from other women and adopting what could be seen as 'masculine' attitudes and behaviour; this inevitably isolates them from female support networks and spills over into their leisure lives, which can become equally circumscribed. Cockburn's (1985) study of women and new technology underlines the extent to which men may feel threatened when women enter areas that have been traditionally male, with a technical competence equal to their own. She suggests that gendering 'works' partly by ascribing a series of polarised characteristics to the 'masculine' and the 'feminine'. Women's feminine nature fits them for the 'soft' aspects of paid work, but a crisis occurs when men need to lay claim to both mental and manual superiority. In terms of their strong identification with 'hard' areas such as physical engineering, men may dismiss intellectual skills and office work as 'soft':

> At the next moment, however, they need to appropriate sedentary, intellectual engineering work for masculinity too. Ideological comple- mentary values such as hard/soft must therefore always be seen as provisional. The values called into play in the hegemonic ideology will vary from time to time and from one situation to another. (Cockburn, 1985, p. 190)

Dominant ideologies are never static, but are constantly undergoing degrees of transformation in relation to changes in associated material conditions. In the same way that lone women entering pubs feel odd, isolated and out of place, the lone woman worker trying to join the male work-group experiences the feeling of being invisible. Wise and Stanley (1987) argue that sexual harassment can operate as a means of maintaining job segregation: the few women who succeed in penetrating male enclaves of highly paid, prestigious jobs are harassed out or harassed into line.

The forms of male control used to exclude women and keep them in their place are remarkably similar in both work and leisure settings. Sexual harassment is typically more overt in traditionally male preserves, and in order to withstand the pressure, women are driven to finding 'coping strategies'. The majority adapt, feeling obliged to make a series of continual adjustments in order to avoid 'trouble'. However, the costs involved in taking this line, if sustained over a lifetime of work, can result in a suppression of spontaneity and sexuality.

Coping strategies vary from avoiding looking directly at people, keeping eyes lowered, and wearing carefully thought-out 'modest' clothes (a strategy adopted by one of the female trainers in imaging technology interviewed by Cockburn), to seeking male sponsorship. The latter technique was reported by Whitehead in her study of rural pubs (1976, p. 176) and Lembright and Riemer (1982) in their study of American women truckers. Trainers in imaging technology were engaged in a considerable amount of travelling and were continually required to enter both work and leisure environments dominated by men. Having 'avoided' troublesome encounters when demonstrating machines in the workplace, they still had to contend with the patriarchal norms of the hotel accommodation provided, where the majority of guests were businessmen.

It is in the area of sexual harassment that class divisions between women can sometimes explain the form that such harassment takes, but not the level or frequency. Faced with such situations, women of all classes are forced to decide between coping strategies, which may include merging with the men and becoming 'one of the boys', or maintaining a female presence, despite the likely outcome of higher visibility and negative male responses. Given such high costs it is unsurprising that most women engage in avoidance rather than confronting patriarchal attitudes and values.

Women's networks: support or control?

A further aspect of the social control process discussed above concerns the role of other women in defining and maintaining 'appropriate' behaviour for women. A substantial amount of research documents the extent and importance of support that women receive from women friends and kin, both domestically and in the workplace (Whitehead, 1976; Delamont, 1980; Pollert, 1981; Westwood, 1984), but these female networks can also be powerful reinforcers of the system of patriarchal control. Women whose behaviour is seen to fall outside the limits of 'normal respectability' are open to sanctions from both men and women, which often take the form of gossip or ostracism. Women's family-based networks, typically forged in joint upbringing and socialisation and maintained through later joint concerns such as childrearing and domesticity, can provide support and identification, but often at a price. Whitehead argues that although the 'women's world' is a source of support, its 'secretness' could be seen as an indication of their powerlessness. Also, it cannot be seen as a counterbalance to patriarchal control when men in the community also have access to kin networks and make as much, if not more, use of them. The mother-daughter tie tends to be one based on exchange of domestic help, rather than joint outings or leisure interests. According to Whitehead, parents, and in particular mothers, become involved in the marital problems of their offspring, typically supporting the marital bond when offering advice or interference. Young wives who attempted to establish more freedom from husband and home were rarely encouraged by their mothers, who had long since given up that particular struggle. Mothers and daughters are unlikely to share the same values, and the former may be restrictive rather than supportive of a daughter's freedom – albeit for the 'best of reasons', namely to avoid 'trouble'. Older women may be acutely aware of the potential consequences of confronting long-established patriarchal values such as physical violence, especially if the confrontation is launched from a position of economic dependence. Whitehead is sceptical about the strength of women's networks as a source of alternative values and the strength for 'fighting back' against male dominance, suggesting that there is a lack of physical basis for such solidarity given that women rarely meet in single-sex groups outside the home in venues where solidarity and support might flourish. Such meetings tend to occur in public settings where displays of female solidarity are viewed as deviant and sometimes threatening (Hey, 1986, pp. 6–7). Instead the women in her study developed what she refers to as 'accommodatory ideologies' (p. 198) which entrench them further in deference and powerlessness.

A similar form of 'collusion' or consent emerges in Westwood's account of the domestic lives of the factory workers at StitchCo, where few of the women attempted to confront an unequal domestic division of labour. This was partly due to their strong identification with the roles of wife and mother and the consensus that domestic labour and childcare were women's 'real work', which provided them with respect and earned approval from others. Westwood notes that any hint of criticism of this from her

> sent them springing to the defence of husbands and children. Husbands were 'good' men because they brought their money home regularly, and didn't get drunk and beat up their wives and children on Friday nights. (Westwood, p. 169)

The role of the extended family in controlling young women via the influence of older female kin is also visible in other cultures, as

Westwood's material on Indian women working in the factory makes clear. (Westwood deliberately uses the term 'Indian' rather than Asian women because it was the term they used to describe themselves.) In Asian households all women are subject to the restrictions imposed by maintaining the family honour (see Chapter 4 and Wilson, 1978), and young women are subject to particularly close surveillance. The gossip and ostracism mentioned above as social control techniques are extensively used among Asian women as an effective self-policing system; at StitchCo older women were frequently the sternest critics of the younger women.

The way in which informal networks operate, especially female ones, effectively to limit the nature and extent of women's leisure is also backed up by data from the Sheffield study, although responsibility for childcare and domestic labour, combined with lack of access to economic resources, constituted the major constraints on women's free time. Men's refusal to contribute to domestic tasks or co-operate with childcare arrangements were two of the most commonly reported means by which they effectively restricted women's access to time and space for leisure. The fact that 97 per cent of the married women interviewed in the survey did the major part of the housework themselves made them well aware of the restrictions on their opportunities for leisure. Added to this, the influence of dominant ideologies about the centrality of 'mothering' in women's lives meant that those women with young children had few choices about restricting their activities to conform with the mothering role. One 22 year old women interviewed at the pilot stage of the Sheffield study remarked: 'As soon as I'd had my baby I felt different, I didn't feel as though I could go to a nightclub' (Green, Hebron and Woodward, 1987c, p. 83). Even when women did manage to create the opportunity for independent leisure, going out without their male partners exposed them, at worst, to the possibility of male violence, and at best to close scrutiny of their behaviour. Contemporary Western society still clings to the premise that married women are the property of one man, their husband. By entering certain public spaces without her husband or a suitable substitute, a woman is perceived to have given up her entitlement to the protection of one particular man, and instead is assumed to be sexually available and hence becomes prey to the advances of any man. Men's objections to women partners going out socially without them are based upon recognition of the above patriarchal norms and codes of practice, as is evident in the reported behaviour of one of the husbands in the Sheffield study:

> I've been in a pub and when he's in uniform he's not supposed to come in, you know, come in for a drink – and I've said I'm going in this particular pub in town and he's come in and said: 'Oh I've just come for a coke. Never drunk a coke in his life, you know, but he'll come and have a coke. He's done that twice on me. (Green, Hebron and Woodward, 1987c, p. 85)

Conclusion: social control as a 'normal' feature of women's daily lives

It seems that in addition to the direct regulation or coercion of women into attitudes and behaviour commensurate with patriarchal norms, men also benefit from women's close supervision of each other. Furthermore, it could be argued that this type of female control based on the implicit acceptance of dominant (male) norms is particularly effective. If women are perceived to be controlling themselves and/or each other, the patriarchal nature of the control is obscured, which often renders the use of more transparent repressive forms unnecessary (Green, Hebron and Woodward, 1987c). Much of the social control of women's behaviour, relying as it does upon norms about respectability, can to a large extent be regarded as control through 'consent' rather than coercion. However, as discussed above, feminist work in the area of women and violence (Hanmer and Saunders, 1984; Stanko, 1985) clearly demonstrates that should this tacit control falter, men have a range of more directly coercive methods of regulating women's behaviour. Women's leisure is effectively circumscribed by male control, male leisure and patriarchal ideas about appropriate activities and venues for women, as well as being linked to age, sexual orientation, ethnicity, income and class (Deem, 1986a).

A key point that emerges from feminist theories of social control and available empirical data, is the extent to which male social control of women is unexceptional; it is a part of normal, everyday life. Most often such control is perceived by both men and women as 'natural' and legitimate, particularly within marriage, with husbands being seen as entitled to govern their wife's behaviour and to punish improper conduct. Women are not free to come and go as they please; if they attempt to do this and neglect or refuse male sponsorship, they may be labelled as irresponsible and 'asking for trouble'. This has clear implications for how, when and where women spend their leisure time and is a major factor in promoting and perpetuating gender inequalities in leisure.

7

Self-help and good practice: the struggle for women's leisure

Introduction

Earlier chapters have analysed the constraints on women's access to free time and limitations on the range of choices available to them about how to spend it – limitations which derive from their structural position in the family and the labour market, and the associated norms and ideologies about 'a woman's place'. Inequalities in childcare and the domestic division of labour, as well as in wage rates for women's and men's work, and in the distribution of personal spending money within the household, all contribute to women's recreational disadvantage. This is reflected to some extent in gender differences in leisure within the home: although the most popular activities such as watching television, listening to music and reading are done by approximately the same proportions of women and men, those which cost money for equipment and require space and time free from interruptions (such as hobbies, crafts and arts) are done by four times as many men as women (see Chapter 4). Men have more leisure time at their disposal than women (Shaw, 1986), women's leisure is much more adversely affected than men's by marriage and parenthood, and the 'quality' of their free time is likely to be reduced by domestic commitments (Green, Hebron and Woodward, 1987b). Gender differences are much more marked for leisure activities away from home, with many more men than women regularly 'going out for a drink' or playing sport. The 1983 *General Household Survey* found that two-thirds of men, compared with under half the women, had been out for a drink in the preceding month. Well over half the men but barely a third of the women had taken part in any sport in the same period (GHS, 1985).

Differences of this magnitude in men's and women's recreational activities have led to the labelling of women as a problem group by policy-makers. In attempts to provide 'official' explanations of women's low participation rates in activities outside the home, public agencies refer to women as recreationally 'disadvantaged' (Department of the Environment) or 'socially and geographically deprived' (Sports Council and Social Science Research Council Joint Working Party on Recreational Research) (see Talbot, 1979, p. 1). As argued in Chapter 1, feminist theorists reject this perception of women as a neglected group whose problems are capable of resolution through piecemeal changes in social policy, and are therefore critical of campaigns such as that organised by the Sports Council to promote women's participation in sport (Stanley, 1980). In Britain the Sports Council is the main arm of government policy in the field of physical recreation, with an annual budget of about £30 million (at 1986 prices). In 1982 it published a major policy document setting out its strategy for the 1980s (Sports Council, 1982). This identified women as a 'target group' whose participation they wished to see increased by 70 per cent for indoor sport and 35 per cent for outdoor sport by 1993. Such a designation of women as a 'target group' encountered resistance from those who argued that women could not be considered 'a group' in the sense of sharing a homogeneous set of recreational preferences, nor were they 'a target' in the sense of being something to be shot at (Brackenridge, 1987a). Talbot has similar reservations:

> What worries me about [The Sports Council's strategy] is that having identified women as an under-participant group, and in some cases referred to them as 'sports illiterate', 'recreationally inert', it means that women themselves are labelled in such a way that people wear blinkers about the way in which they think of them. This goes back to the whole question of stereotype. (Sports Council, 1984, p. 164)

The proposals offered by the Sports Council to reduce the gender imbalance in sports centre use (two male to every female user) and the use of swimming pools (three male to every two female users) include better local provision, 'more suitable' activity programmes, the provision of creches, timings better related to childcare and family timetables, and the 'provision of opportunities to be sociable in surroundings comfortable enough to compete with the pub, the bingo hall, or the back garden fence' (Sports Council, 1982, p. 28). This approach represents progressive thinking in so far as it seeks to offer women recreational opportunities in forms likely to promote their capacity to take advantage of them. However, the document as a whole, its policies and recommendations, and many of the schemes which this strategy has spawned, represent very much a 'top down' approach to the promotion of women's leisure opportunities. It embodies white, male, middle-class, middle-aged professional recreation policy-makers' view of women's needs, namely that provision should be local, 'suitable', timed to fit in with domestic commitments, and 'comfortable'. The report fails to consider issues of gender-based financial inequalities or women's personal security, both within the leisure venue and between it and home. Within professional recreation management circles the provision of a crèche tends to be a knee-jerk response to the issue of adapting the facilities on offer in order to meet women's needs better, and hence to improve women's participation rates in physical recreation (Lloyd, in Sports Council, 1986). Such provision may well be very important for the mothers of pre-school children, but the needs of women as a whole are much more likely to be met by the provision of women-only sessions, or safe transport to and from leisure venues, so that women can try new activities and develop their physical prowess free from male scrutiny and harassment. To deal with these issues, however, is to begin to challenge the sexual *status quo*, as opposed to merely tinkering with its minor manifestations. As Brackenridge has pointed out, organised recreation has become incorporated into the state apparatus for social regulation and control. Agents of the state – in this case, the Sports Council, – determine 'what counts as recreation', and exclude from their policies and practices cultural forms which deviate in style or values from those sanctioned by the dominant social groups. Thus their funding policies reflect the perceptions and interests of white, middle-class males.

At local level the same androcentric thinking is apparent in the failure of many local authority recreation departments to initiate schemes to promote women's leisure (MackSmith and Stewart, 1984); in the difficulties experienced by many facility managers in responding to such initiatives (Bradford Women's Keep Fit and

Sports Group, 1986); and in the difficulties experienced by women and girls in establishing their entitlement, and the privacy and space, to engage in their own physical recreation (London Borough of Hackney, 1987).

The official ideology of women as 'recreationally disadvantaged' is translated into practices and policies at grassroots level which, on the whole, do little to confront the assumptions that are deeply embedded in sports practice and media representations of sport – that it is a masculine activity. The focus of much of this book is on the constraints that restrict women's leisure opportunities. Taken together, this may convey an unduly negative view of women's capacity to enjoy themselves (although it does seem easier to do so in some leisure sites than others). In this chapter we will be examining the ways in which women create opportunities for sociability and enjoyable relaxation within their daily lives. We identify some of the organised forms of 'self-help' that women have established, and conclude with an analysis of what constitutes 'good practice' in promoting women's leisure opportunities, focusing in particular on the situation of two groups of women who experience particular difficulty in enjoying autonomous leisure outside the home, namely the mothers of young children, and Asian women.

Women's informal sociability

Women's capacity to develop and maintain friendships at school, in the workplace, outside the school gates, at the shops and bus stop, and in any number of other unpromising leisure venues where women meet regularly, has long been noted by observers. From the Edwardian wash-house where women gathered to do their laundry, through the door-steps of Bethnal Green, to the factory canteen and teenage bedrooms of the present day, come accounts of close woman-to-woman relationships that provide the emotional, and sometimes material, support which makes life worth living.

Having outlined in an earlier chapter the often restrictive nature of the female support offered to women by relatives and friends, it is equally important to emphasise both the close identification which emanates from that source, and the sheer pleasure women can experience from the company of other women. Fiction and biography are traditionally a rich source of accounts of women's friendship networks, and so too, more recently, is feminist literature which crosses the boundaries between the novel and academic writing (Cartledge and Ryan, 1983; Oakley, 1984; Heron, 1986). These works offer vivid accounts of women's interactions, dealing with issues ranging from the intimate details of personal relationships to the complex issues connected with paid work. These topics are explored and exchanged wherever women meet, with both spheres being accorded equal status and consideration. Generations of women have been well aware of the overlap for them between areas traditionally labelled separately at work, leisure and family life (Clark, 1968; Llewelyn Davies, 1978). Feminist writers have been recently exploring this overlap, documenting the strengths and skills that women gain from operating simultaneously in a number of spheres, rather than, as other literary and 'expert' sources have done, comparing them unfavourably with the one-dimensional skills displayed by many men, as they participate in employment, politics or culture.

Female relatives and neighbours

Kin and neighbours remain significant sources of women's close relationships with each other. Female support networks have always operated within the 'private' sphere of family life and motherhood (Young and Willmott, 1957; Green and Parry, 1982), and it is often during the spaces between work and childcare, where leisure in the form of 'tea and talk' occurs, that the strongest friendships are formed and nurtured. Whilst there may be clear class and ethnic differences, which mediate both the form and subject of this support and advice passed between women, the core of that process is undeniably the shared experience of domestic labour and childcare, and relationships with male partners.

The question of motherhood constitutes an overwhelmingly central force in the lives of women, including those women who remain childless through choice or for reasons of biology. In a society where women are represented primarily as mothers, the spectre and reality of children dominate their lives in a way which generates irritation and denial, as well as pleasure and satisfaction. These 'nurturing' qualities which women are assumed to possess, whether by biology or socialisation, and which are reflected in their roles as wives, mothers and daughters, are important features of their relationships with each other, and demonstrate a recognition of the strong cultural bonds between mothers and daughters. There is both the fear of ending up within the constraints and privations characteristic of their own mothers born a generation earlier (Friday, 1979) and the recognition that mothers are often at the centre of their lives:

> In black families, our mothers are the lynch-pins. Our traditions around food, clothes and ways of working come from our mothers. They're the ones who really organise family life. (Bryan, Dadzie and Scafe, 1985, p. 196)

Spending time with other women and their children can be a major leisure activity for mothers (Deem, 1986a; Wimbush, 1986; Green, Hebron and Woodward, 1987b). Leisure for this group of women is largely home-based and shared with female friends or kin, apart from the occasional night out with male partners or 'the girls'. The context of such leisure time with women re-affirms the bonds of shared experience in the form of discussion of relationships, domestic life and childrearing; stories are swapped and support is offered, thereby maintaining solidarity. Shared expeditions outside the home may only involve trip to the park or the shops, but it is the quality, rather than the formal status of the experience, that is important. This is illustrated by the following comment from a lone parent in the Sheffield study:

> They [women friends] mostly live on here. It's funny because it seems to be a community of one-parent families . . . the days when they're [the children] at school we just sort of decide what we're going to do, go off down town or go for a sauna. (Green, Hebron and Woodward, 1987b, p. 47)

Wimbush's study of the mothers of young children in Edinburgh highlights the significance of 'shared understandings' with other mothers. One of her respondents described the main aspects of this collective identity:

> I feel more at home in some ways being with all women . . . I feel they understand, I think, particularly as most of them are in the same situation as me, I feel they're not criticising me. I sometimes feel that other people think you're incompetent if they're looking at you and think, 'I could do

much better than her. If it was my child it wouldn't throw a tantrum.' . . . Other mothers understand on the whole . . . It's quite restful being with other people who understand. (Wimbush, 1986, p. 114)

The neighbourhood is the primary location for the formation of friendships with other mothers, and Wimbush identifies the street, local shops, nurseries, schools, health centres, community centres and other interest-groups as playing an important role as meeting places, and in promoting sociability. Just as for the older women described by Hunt in Chapter 5, neighbours are an important source of support and leisure companionship. Husbands' absence at work or indifference to their wives' leisure needs if at home make other mothers a vital aid to their own participation in recreation activities away from home. Having a neighbour to go with or to meet at a leisure venue, being able to share childcare, or knowing that someone will call to find out why a 'regular' is missing, are important motivators to the mothers' regular attendance at leisure activities.

Hunt's (1980) study highlights the continuing importance of 'neighbouring' for women beyond the early years of motherhood. She describes life in a mining community where, as in the one studied a quarter of a century earlier by Dennis, Henriques and Slaughter (1969), male bonds forged in the dark and dangerous world of the pit-bottom are crafted and polished in the male world of the working men's club, over a few pints of beer. If husband-wife relationships are highly segregated, instrumental and lacking in emotional warmth, then close ties with female relatives and neighbours provide women with both affection and practical support at a day-to-day level. Hunt describes the friendship between neighbours Muriel and Gladys: they do their laundry together on Saturdays, spend their evenings together at each other's homes, provide childcare for each other, and help with ingredients and cooking for special occasions.

Women as workmates

The location of women's paid employment is another significant source of close friendships between women, as Chapter 5 indicated. Cavendish's (1982) study of women assembly-line workers in a

London factory describes the 'warm and supportive' atmosphere there. The women had a sense of solidarity: 'Friendliness towards all the other women in the shop was automatic – because you were all in the same boat, doing the same work in the same place' (p. 56). This friendly climate encouraged shy women to become more out-going. The women helped each other 'on the line' when one of them was falling behind in her work; they took a concerned interest in the health and personal lives of their workmates; they helped new-comers with their work and introduced them to the other women ; and this sense of womanly community manifested itself in easy verbal and physical contact:

> Even when the work didn't force you to be in direct physical contact, like during the breaks, the women always wanted to sit together . . . They liked to be with people the whole time, and weren't at all used to being on their own. (p. 57)

McNally's (1979) study of women in routine clerical work also relates the formation of workplace friendship groupings to features of the work itself. The 'temps' (temporary clerical staff) formed one such group on the basis of their common discontent with both the nature of the work they had been allocated, and with the employment agency that had hired them to do it. The permanent staff fell into two distinct cliques organised around different job specifications. The sociability enjoyed by the members of these two groups took place both within work and outside it, with the friendliness of workmates being given as the main reason why the young women on the permanent staff chose to stay in such alienating and tedious jobs. Nearly all of these young women went out together in the evenings to discos, parties or pubs, and special events were marked by appropriate rituals in the office. During McNally's period of fieldwork two girls got married during the same week, one from each clique. She describes the practical joking and celebrations at work that accompanied this status-passage, albeit still divided along clique lines: 'Separated by a distance of only six feet, the two groups sat resolutely at their respective tables and held two different "stag parties" ' (p. 167).

The importance to women of these workplace friendships in making both work itself bearable and the working day more enjoyable, and in providing a source of companions for leisure outside working hours, is recognised by women who no longer have access to such relationships. These friendships are not just to do with making the passage of time more pleasant, but provide women 'with a set of social relationships outside the family, from which women derive a crucial sense of themselves' (Coyle, 1984, p. 6).

Part of Coyle's study of women's experience of redundancy was conducted at Castleford, a coal-mining community in Yorkshire close to the town studied by Dennis *et al.* in the 1950s, and part of 'the very heartland of masculinity' (Coyle, p. 102). The importance of friendships with other women at the trouser factory she studied was, in this context, particularly emphasised:

> We all got on like a family, you know. I think it was the best factory ever. Everyone was so close together and we all got on. I was just happy at Roger Firth. We had a right good set of girls, everybody together, there was unity. (p. 53)

As at the factory studied by Cavendish, this one had mainly recruited new staff by word of mouth, so that the workforce were united not only by long-standing friendships but also in many instances by kinship too. For the women who had been made redundant, the rupture of their close relationships with workmates, which stretched back for years in some cases, was a source of considerable nostalgia and regret. They talked with feeling about the isolation, depression and loss of confidence associated with being confined to the home by their unemployment.

Mothers of young children who are full-time houseworkers may voice the same feelings of regret for the lost camaraderie of their time at work, contrasting it with their current structural isolation from female company, in their home. Under these circumstances contact with others in a similar situation is, as for Cavendish's factory workers, a source of support.

'A girl's best friend'

These vital skills at forming supportive friendships with other women and at creating enjoyable leisure out of whatever resources are to hand, in terms of free time, physical space, companionship and money or equipment, are acquired by girls as part of their socialisation. To some extent this is a product of social control through girls' exclusion from participation in many public forms of leisure, and the success of parental strategies to keep girls at home much more than boys. Various studies have identified the strategies employed by teenage boys to control girls' freedom of movement and leisure. These include the monopolisation of space and facilities in youth clubs, verbal techniques of social control directed at the girls' sexuality and reputations, and the effect that young men's violent behaviour ('trouble') had on girls' parents, of tightening their control on their daughters' mobility (McRobbie, 1978; Nava, 1984; Wood, 1984; Griffin, 1985; Lees, 1986; Griffiths, 1988).

Before puberty these gender divisions are less marked. After it they are widened not only by the imposition of these formal and informal controls on girls' behaviour, but also by parents' expectations that girls will do considerable amounts of domestic work and baby-sitting. McRobbie, Nava, Griffiths and others have noted the high level of domestic labour typically performed by teenage girls, but not their brothers, done as a service for their mothers, or for them and neighbours either unpaid or in return for 'pocket money'. Teenage girls thus have less leisure time at their disposal, earn less money than their male peers do in their jobs (delivering newspapers, or working in supermarkets, off-licences and betting shops) and spend much more time in their own or someone else's home. Those who have left school and are unemployed are especially disadvantaged, their poverty cutting them off from access to the commercial recreation which is such an important part of older adolescents' leisure (Griffiths, 1988). Lack of financial resources, coupled with a high level of parental control over girls' mobility away from home, serve to keep girls close to their homes. Nava cites a recent study of fourteen and fifteen year old girls living in North London: one-sixth of them never went out in the evenings without their parents, and one-third only went out once a week.

These restrictions on girls' freedom of access to leisure outside the home are particularly marked for Asian girls. Notions of female modesty and sexual purity enshrined in *purdah* keep married women at home in traditional households, and similar restrictions are imposed on daughters outside school time. The maintenance of family honour, especially in strict Muslim homes, depends on unmarried daughters' preservation of their 'reputation', which would be sullied if they went out with boys, or even wore 'immodest' clothes, or had friends who smoked or hung around on the street. Some Asian girls do risk parental wrath by going out with boys or with non-Asian female friends, the proportion doing so varying according to the age at which they arrived in Britain and their religion (Wilson, 1978). The Asian girls interviewed by Sharpe (1976) in the London suburb of Ealing were well aware of the greater mobility and recreational opportunities enjoyed by their brothers. The contrast between the freedom of their association with boys and non-Asian girls in school time, and their seclusion at home outside school, is a stark one, especially in comparison with the leisure autonomy allowed to boys.

Afro-Caribbean girls enjoy greater freedom than girls in Asian families, but may have restrictions placed on their mobility in the evenings by parents who are worried about racial harassment (Griffin, 1985). One response is to create new forms of leisure with other black girls, which take place at their own or in each other's homes. Griffiths (1988) describes the activities of the Afro-Caribbean teenage girls in her study as coming closest to the 'bedroom culture' described by McRobbie and Garber (1976). Doing each other's hair in beaded braids was an extremely labour-intensive activity which afforded plenty of time for talking and listening to music, and was an important part of their black identity.

A number of writers have identified the invisibility of girls in studies of youth culture (see Nava, 1984) and noted their marginality in organised youth clubs – places which, one imagines, might be seen by parents as offering a relatively 'safe' form of leisure to their teenage daughters in that it takes place in a specified local venue, normally in the early part of the evening, and under responsible adult supervision. Female membership of youth clubs is lower than male membership, and a close analysis of gender differences in access to their facilities, and in spending on provision for girls and the employment of female youth workers, reveals enormous disparities. Nava explains this marginalisation of girls' concerns, in terms similar to Brackenridge's analysis of state policy for sport (discussed earlier), as a reflection of the masculine focus of the policy-makers and educators of youth workers. A significant issue for the youth service is the historic construction of male working-class youth as a potential source of social disorder. The state and voluntary provision of youth clubs can be seen as a mechanism for the regulation and control of adolescent boys, whereas the family has successfully performed the same function for girls. Girls are less likely to be seen on the streets and, if there, are less likely to behave in a 'troublesome' way. Their leisure time is likely to be spent in their own house or at their friends', while their brothers are more often to be found on the street, or at the club or cafe, 'doing nothing' (Corrigan, 1979). It is not surprising, then, that prime sites for teenage girls' leisure are the bedroom, the bathroom and – at school – in the toilets and the changing room (McRobbie and Garber, op. cit.; Griffin *et al.*, 1982; Scraton, 1987). These are places that can be defended from male intrusion, and offer privacy for the real 'work' of adolescent girls' leisure – learning to manage the contradictions of growing up female.

McRobbie (1978) describes the two main factors which rescue teenage girls from the perception of a bleak and unexciting future: first, the security of the 'best friend' relationship and, second, their (collective) immersion in the ideology of romance. Both of these, together with the physical construction of femininity by means of cosmetics, hair products and other consumer durables, take place in spaces which girls can legitimately appropriate, at home or in school:

> In schools toilets are used as somewhere to escape from the classroom and teachers, for trying out make-up, smoking and, most important of all, for talking. Talking for girls and women is not simply relaxation, but is certainly about managing contradictions and gaining support, and its centrality to girls' leisure is not surprise. They (rightly) see talking as positive, sorting out problems with friends, establishing their own space and time. (Griffin *et al.*, 1982, p. 104)

In adolescence, as in adult life, a common and highly valued form of female leisure is the maintenance of social relationships with other women. It is invisible to recreation policy-makers and is unlikely to be recognised as 'leisure' by the women themselves, if asked to give an account of their activities. It may be denigrated as 'gossiping', 'chatting', 'neighbouring' or 'calling' by men, yet provides many girls and women with some pleasure and autonomy within the contexts of their lives. If access to leisure away from home is made problematic by lack of money for transport or recreational spending; if girls and women are kept at home by the demands of children and husbands, or the control of parents; if girls and women fear to travel away from home after dark because of the possibility of sexual or racial attack by men, or are not allowed to do so, because of worries about attacks by men; then this home-based or workplace focus for women's leisure can be no surprise. Rather than seeing female sociability as a 'poor relation' to commercially produced forms of recreation, let us celebrate the enjoyment, support and solidarity afforded by 'having a laugh with the girls'.

Self-help via formal organisations

Women's resourcefulness in creating opportunities for enjoyable leisure by informal means is matched by their energy and activism in formal voluntary organisations. Slightly more women than men are active in clubs, societies, leisure classes and voluntary work (GHS, 1985). These voluntary organisations very often have single-sex membership, whether formally (as for Women's Institutes and Townswomen's Guilds) or tacitly (as in the case of dressmaking, cake decoration or flower-arranging classes). Their activities normally take place regularly, in the same place, and tend to be finished by mid-evening. This makes them 'safe' and socially acceptable places for women to spend their leisure time. The vast majority of evening class students are women, many of them liberated from their childcare responsibilities by the presence of husbands. As Roberts (1978) has pointed out, 'The night school has been one of the few respectable "nights out" for women unaccompanied by husbands and boyfriends.'

But to gain access to this form of leisure can involve women in negotiating their way around various sets of constraints. Deem (1986a) asked a Women's Institute member if her husband minded her being a member. She replied:

> No – not really – he thinks I won't get up to any mischief while I'm here – mind, I have to leave everything just so . . . meal ready to eat when he comes in . . . house tidy . . . kids doing their homework upstairs . . . or it's murder when I get back . . . when *he* goes out to the pub *he* never asks me if I can manage while he's out – it just wouldn't occur to him. (p. 33, original emphasis)

Other women highlighted their difficulty in keeping a regular time slot free of family commitments:

> When you're talking about the kinds of activities that are organised . . . it means they'll be at specific times – say Thursday at 8 o'clock for two hours – well when you've got a family you can't commit yourself to that – you never know what's going to happen on a Thursday night at 8 . . . several times in the past few years I've enrolled in evening classes and in the end I've had to drop out. (Dixey and Talbot, 1982, p. 72)

Several mothers of young children with unemployed husbands interviewed in the Sheffield study were enthusiastic participants in classes run by the local authority. These were local and cheap, and a day-time creche was available. Like the other women quoted, however, their participation was conditional on them having made arrangements for meals and childcare. The contrast between their male partners' leisure, based on the pub and club or around male activities such as fishing and snooker, and their own out-of-home leisure based on these classes, was striking. They differed in cost, timing, and the predictability of their location and the participants' companions. The men's leisure was much more autonomous and required a minimal level of domestic organisation to make it possible, compared with that of their wives. The effort of attending the classes was definitely considered worthwhile:

> I had some great times at night school . . . we really had fun . . . there was a right good bunch of women that all got on together. The teacher was smashing and we learnt a hell of a lot. (Dixey and Talbot, 1982, p. 73)

Some writers have identified these classes as being predominantly middle-class activities. Recent increases in charges may disbar women with little or no spending money from taking part; transport difficulties and extremely localised 'mental maps' can prevent working-class women from travelling beyond their immediate vicinity; and some women identify an 'us' and 'them' divide between middle-class, better educated participants and themselves (Dixey and Talbot, 1982). Deem queries this perception. Although women may have to create their own opportunities to attend classes within the framework of their domestic commitments, with the organisational structure of adult education being perceived by some as a bastion of male privilege and control (Thompson, 1983), such classes can represent an avenue of personal liberation for women. Classes on domestic skills may serve to reinforce rather than threaten the sexual division of labour, but those which expose women to new sets of critical ideas, and develop their insight and self-confidence, can serve fundamentally to undermine 'the structures and beliefs upon which those households were organised' (Deem, 1986a, p. 58).

Women's clubs and organisations, like classes, are an important part of their leisure activity. Their membership tends to be composed of older women, and many clubs are divided along class lines (especially if measured in terms of their male partners' social class affiliation, as in the case of women's organisations associated with Rotary, the Freemasons, Working Men's Clubs, Friendly Societies, and some sports clubs). Although women's role in many of them is formally subordinate to the parallel organisations for men, and often involves them in the provision of traditionally female, socially invisible, supporting services, such as fund-raising and tea-making (see Dempsey, 1987), it is vital to recognise their significance to the women themselves. Their ostensible function is often much less important than the opportunities for sociability and the support and companionship of other women, which they offer in a forum that is socially approved and a legitimate place for women to be.

A major part of many people's recreation involves sport, an area where the subordination of women has been and remains most conspicuous. The Sex Discrimination Act of 1975 specifically excludes sport and private clubs from its sphere of statutory regulation. Consequently some of the most striking examples of both localised and widespread, systematic discrimination come from women's experiences with sports clubs and media coverage of women's sport. Women's response has been to challenge discrimination by mounting campaigns in specific areas, such as attempting to obtain full membership rights for women in working men's clubs, including access to snooker tables (see Rogers, 1984), and to establish equity in golf clubs and bowls clubs. They have also formed organisations with a broader campaigning function, to challenge gender stereotyping and discrimination of women's sport in the media and in sports participation across the board, from schools and clubs to elite level. The Women's Sports Foundation was set up in 1984 on similar lines to a successful organisation of the same name in the United States, with a brief to promote equal opportunities for women in sport through lobbying, promoting conferences, and disseminating information. Its membership is confined to women, but is open to those involved in physical recreation at all levels and across all sports. The links between politics and sport, vehemently denied by elite sportsplayers in defending their right to play in South Africa a few years ago, now seem to have become incorporated into accepted wisdom (Hain, 1982). However, sexism and racism in sport seem to be more difficult for policy-makers and sports administrators to accept. The administration of organised sport is predominantly a white, male, middle-class affair, the same being true of sports coaching (White, 1987; Brackenridge, 1987b). In voluntary sports participation, and increasingly in physical education in schools, men are determining how girls and women should engage in physical recreation activities (Scraton, 1986). Given the neglect of women's elite sport on television and in the press, and the presentation of what little coverage there is emphasising female sexual attractiveness rather than their physical performance, women's lower sports participation rates compared to men should come as no surprise. If sport is portrayed as a masculine activity, the attainment of excellence by girls becomes abnormal and 'unfeminine' (Hargreaves, 1985).

In this hostile environment girls' and women's participation in sport provides opportunities not only for them to escape the confining corset of dominant ideologies which construct feminine appearance and behaviour in narrow stereotypes, but also to form close friendships with other women based on their common interests. The women's sports team of the 1980s probably has as much fun as the school hockey team of the 1960s or the Women's Health and Beauty group of the 1940s did, but today's women are likely to be much more politically aware and active, particularly if they participate at the top level of competitive sport.

What can be done? Good practice in leisure provision

The introduction to this chapter contained a criticism of the 'top down' approach adopted by the English Sports Council in its strategy for promoting women's participation in physical recreation (and that of other 'recreationally disadvantaged' groups). If it achieves little else, this book should have succeeded in demonstrating that the 52 per cent of the population who are female by no means constitute a homogeneous group, with the same recreational preferences and needs. The social and economic categories that divide the population in terms of class, wealth, age group, ethnicity and regional location, as well as divisions associated with family situation, marital status, employment and state of physical health, clearly differentiate groups of women from each other. The forms of sociability most enjoyed by the elderly middle-class women residents of a south-coast town studied by Jerrome (1984) – namely charity work, classes and voluntary associations – have little in common with the leisure of the Yorkshire teenage girls studied by Griffiths (1988). Their gender may place them in a similar structural position in terms of their direct or indirect economic dependence on men's earnings, their relation to the labour market and their sense of security outside the home, but their attitudes and expectations may be vastly different. Thus it follows that official and formal attempts to promote women's leisure opportunities need to take account of the significant differences between various groups of women, in addition to tackling those problems that affect all women to a greater or lesser extent, such as issues about personal security and physical self-confidence. Groups of women that have been identified as subject to particularly acute constraints on their opportunities for leisure away from home are the mothers of pre-school children, and Asian women. It is worth looking in some detail at ways in which these constraints can be tackled through appropriate social policy initiatives and recreational provision to enhance women's leisure opportunities.

Mothers of pre-school children

Studies of the mothers of small children in Edinburgh (Wimbush, 1986) and Sheffield (Green, Hebron and Woodward, 1987b) have identified a range of problems which operate as serious constraints on women's access to free time, the frequency and predictability of its timing, and their freedom to engage in recreation away from home. Shortage of personal spending money, transport difficulties, the lack of leisure companions and the inflexibility of small children's schedules for eating and sleeping all combine to restrict these women's participation in organised leisure.

The Sports Council identified mothers with young children as a priority group in its blueprint for the 1980s (Sports Council, 1982), and held a seminar in 1985 on women and sport as part of its efforts to promote women's participation. The seminar's chairman (sic) hoped that it would create a greater awareness of sport in enhancing the quality of life of women and girls; encourage groups to take action to increase women's and girls' participation; and generate policy recommendations for the relevant agencies (Sports Council, 1986, p. 5). During the day's discussion one participant pointed out that the pre-seminar publicity said:

> We regret that children cannot be admitted to the seminar. It may be possible to arrange crèche facilities, if required, but it is hoped that delegates will make private arrangements wherever possible. (Sports Council, 1986, p. 18)

A number of women, the speaker said, had, been disbarred from taking part in the seminar, just as women were excluded from many forms of sport, by this assumption that childcare was their own concern. This point was supported by one of the organisers, who challenged the Sports Council to defend its position, but the chairman closed down discussion of the issue. In a subsequent report on the seminar its main organiser described it as having failed in its aim

> 'to bring together men and women with an interest in increasing women's and girls' participation in sport and recreation in order to identify problems and suggest remedies' . . . She advised members that, regrettably, this objective had not been fulfilled, due, in the main, to members of the fanatical fringe of the feminist movement who had been more interested in debating sexism and racism and who had subsequently distracted the seminar from discussing the broader issues.

One wonders what these broader issues might be! The point of singling out this incident and the official response to it is to highlight the lack of insight on the part of policy-makers concerning the situation of young mothers. Another of the seminar speakers made the same point about recreation providers' attitudes (pp. 23–4). Arnott (1986) provides supporting evidence for this assertion. Despite the sympathetic attitude of senior staff in the Recreation Department of the local authority she studied, this favourable orientation did not get translated into effective action lower down the hierarchy. The predominantly male staff at all levels of the organisation, and an emphasis at lower levels on 'facility management' rather than 'community development' or 'outreach', meant that only token attempts were made to increase women's use of their facilities. She makes a series of specific recommendations for managers, to enable the mothers of young children to have easier access to the facilities on offer. These are:

Make direct contact with women, to ask them what their needs are.

Site facilities near to women's homes. Few women have access to a car during the day, if at all, and public transport is difficult to use with a pushchair and small child.

Choose the right time. The timetables of schools, nurseries and playgroups impose inflexible schedules on mothers.

Make payment easy. Pay-as-you-go, rather than an annual lump sum, enables women to attend when resources and family commitments allow.

Extend concessionary rates. Young families, those on supplementary benefit and single parents should receive the same concessions as the unemployed.

Welcome children. The planning, design and equipment in leisure venues of various types should consider the needs of children and their carers more.

Cater for families. Offer facilities that parents and children can use together, or separately at the same time in parallel sessions.

Boost self-confidence, by having more women-only sessions, using women staff. This is particularly important for women who have been at home bringing up children, and who may have lost confidence through the lack of involvement in activities outside the home.

Arrange for short-term childcare.

The difficulties of transport, time, finance and confidence, and the generally unwelcoming attitude towards children in this country, were identified as major constraints on young mothers' participation in leisure activities outside the home.

A study of women's leisure in Hackney identified many of the same barriers to the recreation of mothers away from their homes (London Borough of Hackney, 1987): lack of crèche provision, poor local provision of facilities, the high cost and poor timing of events for mothers and children, and – above all – the low priority accorded to mothers' and children's needs by recreation facility managers. Problems to do with transport and women's safety on the streets affected this group of women and others, and the lack of information about what services and facilities were available was a further restriction on women's involvement in existing provision. The Recreation and Arts Department of Leicester City Council, which has been in the vanguard of positive action to promote women's and girls' use of its facilities, found in its survey of local authorities that:

> the vast majority of Authorities have failed to recognise the need for women's/girls' recreation provision and therefore, despite the Sports Council's proposals, the overall picture and present position is one of 'laissez faire'. (MackSmith and Stewart, 1984)

A large number of recreation managers are now apparently aware of the importance of crèche provision in promoting the participation of the mothers of young children in the activities they offer, even if only a minority of them are doing much about it (Lloyd, 1985).

Asian women

Chapter 4 included a brief account of the lives and experiences of Asian women in Britain, which was designed to identify the framework of social and cultural constraints and opportunities that affect their leisure. Clearly there are important differences within the Asian community of men's and women's religion and ethnic affiliation, of social class, and occupational group, of their home life before coming to Britain – as agriculturists in rural communities or engaged in urban commerce – as well as in their level of assimilation to white British culture. There are variations in outlook and expectations between women who grew up in the Asian sub-continent or within Asian communities in East Africa, and young Asian women who have grown up in Britain – although these latter may have had extended visits to their parents' communities of origin. These differences should be borne in mind as qualifying the generalisations that follow.

Although as yet we have few first-hand accounts or ethnographic profiles of Asian women's lives in Britain, there are a number of reports and studies of leisure participation schemes designed for Asian women by some of the more enlightened local authority recreation departments, in communities with sizeable Asian populations. A national survey of local authority provision for girls' and women's recreation carried out by Leicester City Council in 1984 (MackSmith and Stewart, 1984) found that only a small minority of authorities had any specific schemes for girls and women at all, and even fewer had any recreational provision designed specifically for Asian women. Most reported that 'this was not a problem in their area' (p. 18), raising the question of who determines what 'a problem' is, and what criteria are emphasised. Some cities and boroughs with considerable numbers of Asian citizens have devised recreation initiatives aimed to promote the participation of Asian women, and written accounts have been produced of schemes in Bradford, Leicester, the London Borough of Hackney, Birmingham and Wolverhampton. Dixey's exemplary report of a scheme in Bradford sums up one of the main issues to be faced by the organisers of such schemes:

> Immigrants from the Asian sub-continent possess a distinctive culture. This presents a dilemma: on the one hand it is desirable to maintain a definite cultural identity in an unfamiliar environment. On the other hand this very distinctiveness does not aid integration or acceptance from the host community. (Dixey, 1981, p. 1)

The dilemma is to decide whether to engage in small-scale social engineering, or in something likely to be more radical and far-reaching in its effects. The participation of Asian women in leisure activities outside their homes is, as Chapter 4 indicated, lower than that of most other social groups in the population. Given that local authority recreation departments have an obligation to try to meet the needs of *all* their local residents, as far as this can be achieved, then special efforts to enable Asian women to engage in leisure away from home can be justified in these terms. It will almost certainly cost more to attract each person in this 'hard-to-reach' group to the facilities on offer than, say, to bring in young, white men, because of additional costs in staffing, transport, publicity in vernacular languages, and the exclusion of other users at specific times. However, if the political will to increase women's leisure opportunities is strong, then some reallocation of resources can be achieved – albeit with possible resistance from the currently advantaged groups whose access to facilities will thereby be worsened (see, for example, reports of resistance to 'women only' sessions: London Borough of Hackney, 1987, p. 36; Pearson, 1986). In the context of prevailing ideologies about the benefits of physical recreation, this policy can be defended as extending access and opportunities to what is perceived as a disadvantaged group. Most of the schemes seem to have adopted this approach. Dixey describes how community workers sought the informed approval of the religious leaders of the Asian community and women's husbands, and took care to offer their services in a way that would make them culturally acceptable.

The specific difficulties facing Asian women, especially those who have grown up within conservative rural communities in Pakistan and Bangladesh, are that they are unlikely to be employed outside the home, because of cultural norms and their limited command of the English language. They are likely to experience social isolation as they try to come to terms with an alien urbanised society whose members can be difficult to communicate with. In addition, the population from the New Commonwealth is highly localised in inner-city areas of 'multiple deprivation'. Housing, recreational facilities and the physical environment are generally worse than elsewhere, and these parts of cities include a disproportionate share of people living in poverty. These material deprivations are exacerbated by the fear of racist attacks. The study of women's leisure in Hackney reports that Asian people living in the borough are fifty times more likely to be attacked than whites, and Afro-Caribbean people are thirty-six times more likely.

The Greater London Council's study of women's mobility (GLC, 1984, 1985) found, via an Asian woman interviewer, that two-fifths of the Asian women respondents knew of other Asian women who had been attacked or harassed in the previous year, and one in five had themselves been attacked. Most of these attacks took place in the street, or whilst travelling or waiting for public transport, and involved thefts or muggings. The harassment mainly involved verbal abuse. None of these incidents had been reported to the police, because (according to the Hackney report, p. 43) of the level of personal institutionalised racism within the police force, and the women's well-grounded expectation that their case would not be treated seriously. The impact of this fear of attack compounds the cultural constraints that confine many Asian women to their homes for much of the time. Less than one Asian woman in ten in the London survey felt safe walking at night, and 95 per cent of the respondents said that they did not go out on their own at night. These concerns are reflected in the Asian women's patterns of leisure-related travel: they were much more likely than the white or Afro-Caribbean women studied to entertain friends and relatives at home or to pay visits to them, and were less likely to go to clubs and classes, to do voluntary work, to play or watch sport, or to engage in other leisure activities away from home (GLC, 1984, p. 5). Because of these problems with travel, several local authority schemes report that door-to-door transport, preferably with a woman driver, was an important part of their planning if Asian women were to be able to avail themselves of the facilities on offer. In the Bradford scheme this had the added 'advantage' (to the women's husbands and to male community leaders) of offering reassurance that 'nothing would take place which offended custom' as 'in effect, therefore, they were in the care of the school for the entire period spent away from home' (Dixey, 1981, p. 3).

This sensitivity to cultural norms and practices is vital to the success of such initiatives. The reports referred to earlier describe schemes for Asian women to attend regular sessions of swimming and keep-fit, or the organisation of ethnic cultural events and festivals. Physical recreation for Asian women raises particular issues about women's clothing; the nature of the physical environment where the activity takes place and the changing rooms; the gender of the instructor and her/his expectations and manner; and also the considerations that apply to any activity away from home, such as contact with non-kin men, the activity's location, and the women's personal safety. All of these need to be carefully considered, and facility staff need to be educated in gender- and race-awareness, to avoid the common complaint of recreation managers, if schemes elicit a poor response, that 'we lay on these sessions, but they don't really want to do it'. The Bradford scheme, which offered Asian women regular opportunities to do swimming and keep-fit exclusively with other Asian women, female instructors, and in a school (which was seen as a legitimate place for the women to go), involved the careful planning of how to deal with all these points.

When such initiatives are successful, they clearly offer groups of Asian women the chance to develop new skills: one year after the beginning of the Bradford swimming project, all of its participants had learned to swim, several had mastered two or three different strokes, and some were learning to dive. Such schemes can be seen as a legitimate reason for women to leave their homes, they offer important opportunities for women to make contact with each other, and can be a forum for learning about other aspects of British society (Dixey, 1981, p. 3). They are clearly enjoyed by some or all of the participants: one report includes an account of a day trip to the Peak District by a group of Asian women from Coventry, and another of a Pakistani woman who was able to take up swimming after a twenty-year break (Rigg, 1986, pp. 81–3). The outcome of these experiences for the women concerned is likely to be greater self-confidence and an expansion of their friendships with other women. It can also contribute to a shift in the balance of power within the household.

It has been suggested that social change, in so far as it affects women's emancipation, may be taking place more slowly within Asian families in Britain than in the Indian sub-continent (Sports Council, 1986). The low status of many Asian men in British society disposes them to be conservative and authoritarian in the home, to reassure themselves that there are still people beneath them in the social pecking order (Dixey, 1981, p. 6). Also, some Asian families may be able to enhance their status and prestige by being more orthodox than others in their religious observance and household mores (Wilson, 1978). Opportunities of the kind described earlier can therefore have an important role in opening up for women alternative evaluations of their personality and position. Asian women in some areas have been involved in activities which educate other ethnic groups about their religion, arts and culture. Many schools in multi-ethnic catchment areas in Britain welcome parents in to talk to pupils about their religious festivals and to help celebrate them, and some local authorities now put up street decorations for Divali as well as Christmas. Others help to fund and promote ethnic cultural events. Women are likely to have a key role in these activities.

Conclusion

Despite creditable localised schemes to promote women's greater involvement in recreation outside the home, which have certainly promoted the well-being and enjoyment of those women who have used the more successful and better designed initiatives, the overall picture looks bleak. The reasons for this are not hard to find. Despite some good intentions on the part of the Sports Council, the labelling of women (or other sections of the population) as having a problem may serve to construct them as a problem. Given the overwhelmingly male composition of recreation management staff at policy-making level, this promotes a blinkered perception of the 'target group' which owes more to stereotyping than it does to the careful identification of what women themselves see as their needs. As Talbot argues, 'the implication is to change women's behaviour to fit sport as it is. This approach reflects what has been called the "add women and stir" approach' (Sports Council, 1984, p. 162).

The development of the philosophy and approach of community recreation would seem to offer the best way forward for promoting women's leisure opportunities. The involvement of local women in the identification of their preferences and needs, and the sensitivity of women staff in helping to effect changes in provision, is having some notable local successes (Rigg, 1986; Warrington and White, 1986). This approach is far more likely to bring about the increased participation by women which the Sports Council is seeking than any 'top down' determination by senior men about the delivery of services, in terms which they decide. Taylor (1986) argues that recreation managers should be accountable and progressive, and not shrink from promoting social change. If a more sensitive and perceptive generation of leisure providers can effectively utilise and promote women's traditional enjoyment of leisure in each other's company, then the future holds excellent prospects for 'a good time to be had by all'!

8
Conclusion

As always, the drawing of conclusions is essentially a retrospective process, which includes reviewing the work that forms the bulk of this book. However, we should also endeavour to identify the likely future directions of leisure in general and for women's leisure in particular. Looking back over our work, what is striking is the enormity of the task we set ourselves. Although we are by no means the first to tackle 'women and leisure', the two areas are so vast that we certainly cannot have told the whole story. This is not false modesty, nor an apologia for our shortcomings, but rather a recognition that there is still much to be done before we fully understand leisure, and women's experiences of it. Leisure is a social process which therefore changes over time. Our concern as feminists continues to be with how to ensure that women are not denied equal access to leisure, whatever its future forms.

The initial premise of our work was to attempt to understand women's experiences of leisure, and to question how far leisure is even a meaningful concept for women. By doing this we also hoped to achieve the important goal of putting women well and truly on the map in the rather narrow field of leisure studies. The apparent male dominance, in terms of approach if not always in terms of the gender of the scholars themselves, had clear implications for the way in which leisure was typically studied. It was separated off as a discrete area of life, predominantly viewed in relation to paid work. Men were the focus of study, by and large. Women, it was assumed, either had the same experiences as men, in which case there was no need to study them, or else they were anomalous and messed up the research findings.

As women and as feminists, we knew that women had to be the focus of our empirical work. We also knew from our own experience, limited as it was, that there was little point in studying leisure as a series of 'activities'. Rather, we wanted to engage with a whole set of social practices which might be incorporated into a broad definition of leisure, set in the context of women's whole lives. Our desire to do this had immediate implications for the way in which we gathered our data. With hindsight, the decision not to question women directly and solely about their 'leisure', but to ask questions about how their time is structured, about their employment and domestic lives, about preferred activities, and so on, proved extremely fruitful. Our attempts to provide feedback to the research subjects as an integral part of the research process was often difficult or expensive in terms of valuable research time, but we would still insist on the importance of breaking down the traditional distance and hierarchy of the researchers *vis-à-vis* the researched. A final conclusion about method relates to the value of being part of a network of researchers – and practitioners – who are concerned with breaking down some of the boundaries of the 'conventional wisdom' (Clarke and Critcher, 1985).

Whilst our own work has necessarily been exploratory rather than hypothesis-testing in nature, we have been convinced that 'leisure' is extraordinarily resistant to being confined to any one, neat definitional category. This might sound like ducking the issue. It would be heartening, at the level of theory, to be able to provide an adequate definition of this amorphous concept. It still frustrates that we have not achieved this. Leisure is a highly personal and subjective mix of experiences. In women's day-to-day lives its definition shifts, is never static, but blurs into and out of other areas of life. Simultaneously, it is also a highly political concept.

This may seem surprising at first sight, given commonsense understandings about leisure and the freedom to choose how one spends leisure time. Looking at the development of leisure as experience and as ideological construction over time is extremely useful in coming to terms with seeing leisure as rather more than individual personal choice. Looking specifically for leisure for women encounters problems, due to the scant documentation of women's leisure *per se*. Fortunately we have been able to make use of some excellent work done by feminist historians on women's experiences more generally. By supplementing these with leisure histories, community studies and so on, we were able to chronicle some of the changes over time and to point to the centrality of some key issues in the development of leisure as we conceptualise and experience it today.

Despite the changing nature of leisure, it has been consistently divided along lines of gender, as well as by class and race. Our work has to a large extent been culturally and geographically specific. However, it seems reasonable to assert that, as in any other fundamentally patriarchal society, British women occupy a socially and economically inferior position. Their material position and prevailing social definitions of masculinity and femininity have a determining effect on the ways in which we understand and live out our lives, including our leisure. For instance, even women who resist prescriptive definitions of femininity, the family and so on, do so in reaction against them. It is impossible simply to ignore them.

The enduring cultural stereotype of women as carers, which for many women is also a reality, has important repercussions. Women's leisure becomes a particularly low priority, both within households and also in society at large. Our own work, in common with that of other researchers in associated fields, has highlighted issues relating to sexuality, respectability and social control as being of the utmost importance *vis-à-vis* women's leisure. We were surprised as we uncovered more and more evidence of the extent to which women's behaviour is constrained, either by ourselves or by others, in response to norms about appropriate female (and male) behaviour. We were also made aware of the variety of strategies that men employ to restrict women's behaviour. Control by men, either individually or collectively, is not only widely practised; it is also widely held to be a normal feature of everyday life.

None of the above are new phenomena; all have strong antecedents. They force us into questioning seriously any definition of leisure as simply freely chosen individual behaviour. So too does taking account of historical shifts in the provision and consumption of leisure. Much of our work has concentrated on individual women's experiences of leisure. However, there is a need to analyse the interplay between leisure and other areas of life, such as education and work, and crucially its role in the economy.

At the level of provision, we have noted the emergence in the nineteenth century of 'rational recreation', a set of beliefs and practices which operate in a paternalistic way to offer the kinds of leisure deemed to 'improve' the lives of those individuals who are less fortunate (read also less educated, less moral, less cultured or civilised) than the provider. Rational recreation as a philosophy has become enshrined in much leisure provision, be it through public subsidy or private patronage. However, women, unlike (working-class) men, were not usually seen as in need of control or direction in their leisure. Given that women have rarely been considered in their own right, they have been far less subject to the kind of leisure provided by the proponents of rational recreation.

Whatever our reservations about such provision, and they are considerable, the important development of the use of public money to finance recreation was a significant feature, and one which might still be used to women's advantage. However, such provision has always been at best marginal, with most people turning to the commercial sector as the major provider of leisure. Not surprisingly, the drive for profit within the commercial sector has seen the public sector lagging behind and often serving to fill in some of the gaps left by the market. Obviously, commercial leisure provision is about the selling of leisure services and goods to consumers who can afford them. For many women, access to money to spend on leisure is limited or non-existent, so the market has not served women particularly well. However, the drive for new markets, increasingly defined in terms of the 'lifestyle' category so beloved of advertisers, has ensured increased and quite imaginative provision for particular groups of women.

Leisure is undergoing a phase of radical restructuring, which has clear implications for the leisure choices that everyone is able to make. State support for the arts, sport and leisure has never had more than a fairly tenuous foothold. but some enlightened work has been achieved, particularly by the more politically progressive local authorities, in terms of broadening access to leisure facilities. At a time when public spending on the most essential provision, namely health, education and housing, is under concerted attack from central government and when the present arts minister, Richard Luce, publicly espouses the notion that 'if it's any good, people will pay for it', what is the future for public leisure provision? Local authorities are selling off their leisure facilities to private companies, libraries are having to consider charging users, many galleries, museums and so on have already had to implement charges. Proposals for the deregulation of broadcasting threaten access not only to entertainment but also to essential information. Many women will simply not be able to buy into ever more commodified leisure.

Certainly, the face of leisure provision is changing, and future prospects are not encouraging. But we should remind ourselves that on the whole leisure provision for women has throughout history been extremely partial, and that women's wider social position has made their access to autonomous leisure generally more difficult than for most men. Despite this, and taking for granted that what we want is for women's needs to be met, we did talk to women who are making real inroads into the male bastions of leisure, and to many others who are managing to claim some time, and pleasure, for themselves in the face of very limited resources. This is not to trivialise the very real difficulties and discrimination women face, but simply to ask if we could build on some of these achievements. Perhaps the next stage is to make visible these achievements and to challenge the restricted definitions of leisure that currently hold centre stage.

Bibliography

Abrams, M. (1978) *Beyond Three-score and Ten: A First Report on a Survey of the Elderly* (Mitcham, Surrey: Age Concern).

Abrams, M. (1980) *Beyond Three-score and Ten: A Second Report on a Survey of the Elderly* (Mitcham, Surrey: Age Concern).

Allen, S. and Wolkowitz, C. (1987) *Homeworking: Myths and Realities* (London: Macmillan).

Amos, V., and Parmar, P. (1984) 'Challenging Imperial Feminism', *Feminist Review*, no. 1.

Arnott, A. (1986) 'Leisure Opportunities for Mothers: Who Cares?', *Leisure Management*, September, pp. 17–19

Atkinson, J. (1984) *Flexibility, Uncertainty and Manpower Management*, Institute of Manpower Studies, Report no. 89.

Aubrey, P., Herbert, D., Carr, P., Chambers, D., Clark, S. and Cook, F. (1986) *Work and Leisure in the 1980s: The Significance of Changing Patterns* (London: Sports Council).

Ballard, R. (1982) 'South Asian Families', in Rapoport, R., Fogarty, M. and Rapoport, R. (eds) *Families in Britain* (London: Routledge and Kegan Paul).

Barker, D. Leonard and Allen, S. (eds) (1976a) *Dependence and Exploitation in Work and Marriage* (London: Longman).

Barker, D. Leonard and Allen, S. (eds) (1976b) *Sexual Divisions and Society* (London: Tavistock).

Barrett, M. (1980) *Women's Oppression Today* (London: Verso).

Barrett, M. (1985) 'Ideology and the Cultural Production of Gender', in Newton, J. and Rosenfelt, D., *Feminist Criticism and Social Change* (London: Methuen).

Barrett, M. and McIntosh, M. (1985) 'Ethnocentrism and Socialist-Feminist Theory', *Feminist Review*, no. 20

Barrow, J. (1982) 'West Indian Families: An Insider's Perspective', in Rapoport, R. *et al.* (eds) *Families in Britain* (London: Routledge and Kegan Paul).

Beechey, V. (1987) *Unequal Work* (London: Verso).
Beechey, V. and Allen, R. (1983) *U221 The Changing Experience of Women*, Unit 1 (Milton Keynes: The Open University).
Beechey, V. and Perkins, T. (1987) *A Matter of Hours: Women, Part-time Work and the Labour Market* (Cambridge: Polity Press).
Beechey, V. and Whitelegg, E. (1986) *Women in Britain Today* (Milton Keynes: Open University Press).
Bennett, H. T., Martin, M., Mercer, C. and Woollacott, J. (1981) *Culture, Ideology and Social Process*, (London: Batsford).
Berk, R. A. *et al.* (1983) 'Mutual Combat and Other Family Violence Myths' in Finkelhor, D. *et al.*, *The Dark Side of Families: Current Family Violence Research* (Beverley Hills: Sage).
Beuret, K. and Makings, L. (1987) 'Love in a Cold Climate: Women, Class and Courtship in a Recession' in Keil, T., Allat, P., Bytheway, B. and Bryman, A. (eds) *Women and the Life Cycle: Transitions and Turning Points* (London: Macmillan).
Binney, V., Harkell, G. and Nixon, J. (1981) *Leaving Violent Men: A Study of Refuges and Housing for Battered Women* (Women's Aid Federation).
Binns, D. and Mars, G. (1984) 'Family, Community and Unemployment: A Study in Change', *Sociological Review*, vol. 32, no. 4.
Blue, A. (1987) *Grace Under Pressure: The Emergence of Women in Sport* (London: Sidgwick and Jackson).
Brackenridge, C. (1987a) 'Women and Community Recreation in the UK', paper presented at the Congress on Movement and Sport in Women's Life, University of Jyväskylä, Finland.
Brackenridge, C. (1987b) 'Gender Inequalities in Sports Leadership', paper presented at the First International Congress on the Future of Adult Life, Leeuwenhorst, The Netherlands.
Bradford Women's Keep Fit and Sports Group (1986) *Women's Day of Recreation: A Report of the Day and What Went into It*, (Bradford: City of Bradford Metropolitan Council).
Bryan, B., Dadzie, S. and Scafe, S. (1985) *The Heart of the Race: Black Women's Lives in Britain* (London: Virago).
Brown, M. (1974) *Sweated Labour: A Study of Homework*, Pamphlet No. 1 (London: Low Pay Unit).
Burgoyne, J. and Clark, D. (1984) *Making A Go Of It* (London: Routledge and Kegan Paul).
Burgoyne, J. (1985) 'Unemployment and Married Life', Unemployment Unit Bulletin No. 18, November, London.
Burman, S., (ed.) (1979) *Fit Work For Women* (London: Croom Helm).
Cain, M. (1973) *Society and the Policeman's Role* (London: Routledge and Kegan Paul).
Callan, H. (1975) 'The Premiss of Dedication: Notes towards an Ethnography of Diplomats' Wives', in Ardener, S. (ed.) *Perceiving Women* (London: Dent).
Carrington, B. and Leaman, O. (1983) 'Work for Some and Sport for All', *Youth and Policy*, vol. 1., no. 3.

172   *Bibliography*

Cartledge, S. and Ryan, J. (1983) *Sex and Love: New Thoughts on Old Contradictions* (London: The Women's Press).

Cartwright, A. *et al.* (1975) *Designing a Comprehensive Community Response to Problems of Alcohol Abuse* (London: Department of Health and Social Security).

Cavendish, R. (1982) *Women On The Line* (London: Routledge and Kegan Paul).

Centre for Contemporary Studies, Race and Politics Group, (1982) *The Empire Strikes Back: Race and Racism in '70s Britain* (London: Hutchinson).

Clark, A. (1968) *The Working Life of Women in the Seventeenth Century* (London: Frank Cass).

Clarke, J. and Critcher, C. (1985) *The Devil Makes Work: Leisure in Capitalist Britain* (London: Macmillan).

Clutterbuck, D. and Hill, R. (1981) *The Re-Making of Work: Changing Work Patterns and How to Capitalise On Them* (London: Grant McIntyre).

Coalter, F. and Parry, N. (1982) *Leisure Sociology or the Sociology of Leisure!* (London: Polytechnic of North London).

Cockburn, C. (1983) *'Brothers': Male Dominance and Technological Change* (London: Pluto).

Cockburn, C. (1985) *Machinery of Male Dominance: Women, Men and Technical Know-How* (London: Pluto).

Commission for Racial Equality (1981) *Between Two Cultures: A Study of Relationships between Generations in the Asian Community in Britain* (London: CRE).

Cooper, C. and Davidson, M. (1982) *High Pressure: Working Lives of Women Managers* (London: Fontana).

Corrigan, P. (1979) *Schooling the Smash Street Kids* (London: Macmillan).

Coward, R. (1978) 'Sexual Liberation and the Family', *m/f*, no. 1.

Coyle, A. (1984) *Redundant Women* (London: The Women's Press).

Cragg, A. and Dawson, T. (9181) *Qualitative Research Among Homeworkers* Department of Employment Research Paper No. 21 (London: Department of Employment).

Crine, S. (1979) *The Hidden Army* (London: Low Pay Unit).

Crompton, R. and Mann, M. (eds) (1986) *Gender and Stratification* (Cambridge: Polity Press).

Cunningham, H. (1980) *Leisure in the Industrial Revolution* (London: Croom Helm).

Curlee, J. (1968) 'Women Alcoholics', *Federal Probation*, vol. 32.

Davis, A. (1981) *Women, Race and Class* (London: The Women's Press).

Deem, R. (1982) 'Women, Leisure and Inequality', *Leisure Studies*, vol. 1, pp. 29–46.

Deem, R. (1984) 'Paid Work, Leisure and Non-Employment: Shifting Boundaries and Gender Differences', paper presented to the BSA Annual Conference, University of Bradford.

Deem, R. (1986a) *All Work and No Play? The Sociology of Women and Leisure* (Milton Keynes: Open University Press).

Deem, R. (1986b) 'The Politics of Women's Leisure', in Coalter, F. (ed.) *The Politics of Leisure*, conference volume no. 3 of The Leisure Studies Association International Conference on Leisure: Politics, Planning and People.

Delamont, S. (1980) *The Sociology of Women* (London: Allen and Unwin).

Delphy, C. (1977) *The Main Enemy: A Materialist Analysis of Women's Oppression*, Explorations in Feminism No. 3 (London: Women's Research and Resources Centre).

Dempsey, K. (1987) 'Gender Inequality: The Exclusion and Exploitation of Women by Men in an Australian Rural Community', paper presented at the First International Congress on the Future of Adult Life, Leeuwenhorst, The Netherlands, April 1987.

Dennis, N., Henriques, F. and Slaughter, C. (1969) *Coal Is Our Life: An Analysis of a Yorkshire Mining Community* (London: Tavistock).

Dixey, R. (1981) *The Fairfax Project Report* (Leeds: Sports Council, Yorkshire and Humberside Regional Office).

Dixey, R. and Talbot, M. (1982) *Women, Leisure and Bingo* (Leeds: Trinity and All Saints College).

Dobash, R. and Dobash, R. (1980) *Violence Against Wives – A Case against the Patriarchy* (London: Open Books).

Driver, G. (1979) 'Classroom Stress and School Achievement: West Indian Adolescents and Their Teachers', in V. Saifullah Khan (ed.) *Minority Families in Britain: Support and Stress* (London: Macmillan).

Driver, G. (1982) 'West Indian Families: An Anthropological Perspective' in Rapoport, R. *et al.* (eds) *Families in Britain* (London: Routledge and Kegan Paul).

Dunning, E. (ed.) (1971) *The Sociology of Sport* (London: Frank Cass).

Dunning, E. and Sheard, K. (1979) *Barbarians, Gentlemen and Players* (Oxford: Martin Robertson).

Eagleton, T. (1976) *Marxism and Literary Criticism* (London: Methuen).

Edgell, S. (1980) *Middle-Class Couples: A Study of Segregation, Domination and Inequality in Marriage* (London, Allen and Unwin).

Edwards, S. (1987) 'Provoking Her Own Demise: From Common Assault to Homicide', in Hanmer, J. and Maynard, M. (eds) *Women, Violence and Social Control* (London: Macmillan).

Eisenstein, Z. (ed.) (1979) *Capitalist Patriarchy and the Case for Socialist Feminism* (New York: Monthly Review Press).

Family Policy Studies Centre (1985) *The Family Today: Continuity and Change* (London: Family Policy Studies Centre).

Finch, J. (1983) *Married to the Job: Wives' Incorporation in Men's Work* (London: Allen and Unwin).

Finch, J. and Groves, D. (eds) (1983) *A Labour of Love: Women, Work and Caring* (London: Routledge and Kegan Paul).

Fowlkes, M. (1980) *Behind Every Successful Man: Wives of Medicine and Academe* (New York: Columbia University Press).

Frazer, E., Ballaster, R., Beetham, M. and Hebron, S. (forthcoming) *Women's Worlds: Magazines and the Female Reader* (London: Macmillan).

Friday, N. (1979) *My Mother Myself* (London: Fontana).

Fryer, P. (1984) *Staying Power: The History of Black People in Britain* (London: Pluto Press).

Gamarnikow, E., Morgan, D., Purvis, J. and Taylorson, D. (eds) (1983) *The Public and the Private* (London: Heinemann).

Game, A. and Pringle, R. (1984) *Gender at Work* (London: Pluto).

Gelles, R. J. (1980) 'Violence in the Family: A Review of Research in the Seventies', *Journal of Marriage and the Family*, vol. 42, no. 4.

General Household Survey 1973 (1975) (London: HMSO).

General Household Survey 1983 (1985) (London: HMSO).

Gerber, L. (1983) *Married to their Careers: Career and Family Dilemmas in Doctors' Lives* (London: Tavistock).

Gilroy, P. (1987) *There Ain't No Black In The Union Jack* (London: Hutchinson).

Gittins, D. (1985) *The Family in Question: Changing Households and Familiar Ideologies* (London: Macmillan).

Gittins, D. (1982) *Fair Sex, Family Size and Structure 1900–39* (London: Tavistock).

Glyptis, S. and Chambers, D. (1982) 'No Place Like Home', *Leisure Studies*, vol. 1, no. 4.

Goffman, E. (1979) *Gender Advertisements* (London: Macmillan).

Goldthorpe, J., Lockwood, D., Bechhofer, F. and Platt, J. (1969) *The Affluent Worker in the Class Structure* (Cambridge: Cambridge University Press).

Graham, H. (1983) 'Do Her Answers Fit His Questions? Women and the Survey Method', in Gamarnikow, E., Morgan, D., Purvis, J. and Taylorson, D. (eds) *The Public and The Private* (London: Heinemann).

Greater London Council Women's Committee (1984) *Women On The Move: GLC Survey on Women and Transport*, no. 5, *Detailed Results: Black Afro-Caribbean and Asian Women* (London: Greater London Council).

Greater London Council Women's Committee (1985) *Women On The Move: GLC Survey on Women and Transport*, no. 3, *Survey Results: Safety, Harassment and Violence* (London: Greater London Council).

Green, E., Hebron, S. and Woodward, D. (1987a) *Women's Leisure in Sheffield: A Research Report* (Sheffield: Department of Applied Social Studies, Sheffield City Polytechnic).

Green, E., Hebron, S. and Woodward, D. (1987b) *Gender and Leisure: A Study of Sheffield Women's Leisure* (London: The Sports Council).

Green, E., Hebron, S. and Woodward, D. (1987c) 'Women, Leisure and Social Control' in Hanmer, J. and Maynard, M. (eds) *Women, Violence and Social Control* (London: Macmillan).

Green, E. and Hebron, S. (1988) 'Leisure and Male Partners' in Wimbush, E. and Talbot, M. (eds) *Relative Freedoms* (Milton Keynes: Open University Press).

Green, E. and Parry, J. (1982) 'Women, Part-time Work and the Hidden Costs of Caring', paper presented to the BSA Annual Conference, University of Manchester.

Green, E. and Woodward, D. (1977) 'The Treatment of Women in Industrial Sociology Texts', paper presented to the British Sociological Association Industrial Sociology Group, Imperial College, London.

Green, E. and Woodward, D. (1988) 'Not Tonight Dear: The Social Control of Women's Leisure', in Wimbush, E. and Talbot, M. (eds) *Relative Freedoms* (Milton Keynes: Open University Press).

Green, E., Woodward, D. and Hebron, S. (1988) 'Leisure, Lifestyles and Women's Work: An Examination of the Implications of Recent Labour Market Changes for Women's Leisure', paper presented to the Leisure Studies Association Second International Conference on Leisure, Labour and Lifestyles, University of Sussex.

Green, E. and Woodward, D. (1989) 'Women's Leisure Experiences in Sheffield', paper presented to Science '89, the British Association's Annual Conference, University of Sheffield and Sheffield City Polytechnic.

Gregory, S. (1982) 'Women Amongst Others: Another View', *Leisure Studies*, vol. 1, no. 1.

Griffin, C. (1981) 'Young Women and Leisure', in Tomlinson, A. (ed.) *Leisure and Social Control* (Brighton: Brighton Polytechnic).

Griffin, C., Hobson, D., McIntosh, S. and McCabe, T. (1982) 'Women and Leisure' in Hargreaves, J. (ed.) *Sport, Culture and Ideology* (London: Routledge and Kegan Paul).

Griffin, C. (1985) *Typical Girls; Young Women From School to the Job Market* (London: Routledge and Kegan Paul).

Griffiths, V. (1988) 'From "Playing Out" to "Dossing Out"' in Wimbush, E. and Talbot, M. (eds) *Relative Freedoms: Women and Leisure* (Milton Keynes: Open University Press).

Gross, E. (1961) 'A Functional Approach to Leisure Analysis', *Social Problems*, Summer, pp. 2–8.

Hain, P. (1982) 'The Politics of Sport Apartheid', in Hargreaves, J. (ed.) *Sport, Culture and Ideology* (London: Routledge and Kegan Paul).

Hakim, C. (1987) 'Homeworking in Britain: Key Findings from the National Survey of Home-based Workers', *Employment Gazette*, February.

Hall, A. (1978) *Sport and Gender: A Feminist Perspective on the Sociology of Sport* (Ottawa: Canadian Association for Health).

Hall, C. (1979) 'The Early Formation of Victorian Domestic Ideology', in Burman, S. (ed.) *Fit Work for Women* (London: Croom Helm).

Hall, C. (1982) 'The Butcher, the Baker, the Candlestick Maker: The Shop and the Family in the Industrial Revolution', in Whitelegg, E. *et al.* (eds) *The Changing Experience of Women* (Oxford: Martin Robertson).

Hall, S. (1977) 'Culture, the Media and the Ideological Effect', in Curran, J., Gurevitch, M. and Woollacott, J., *Mass Communication and Society* (London: Edward Arnold).

Hall, S. (1981) 'Cultural Studies: Two Paradigms', in Bennett, H. T. *et al.*, *Culture, Ideology and Social Process* (London: Batsford).

Hall, S. (1984) 'The Culture Gap', in *Marxism Today*, January, Vol. 28, no. 1, pp. 18–24.

Hamilton, R. and Barrett, M. (1986) *The Politics of Diversity: Feminism, Marxism and Nationalism* (London: Verso).

Handy, C. (1984) *The Future of Work: A Guide to a Changing Society* (Oxford: Blackwell).

Hanmer, J. and Saunders, S. (1983) 'Blowing the Cover of the Protective Male: A Community Study of Violence to Women', in Gamarnikow, E., Morgan, D., Purvis, J. and Taylorson, D., *The Public and The Private* (London: Heinemann).

Hanmer, J. and Saunders, S. (1984) *Well Founded Fear: A Community Study of Violence to Women* (London: Hutchinson).

Hanmer, J. and Maynard, M. (eds) (1987) *Women, Violence and Social Control* (London: Macmillan).

Hargreaves, J. (ed.) (1982) *Sport, Culture and Ideology* (London: Routledge and Kegan Paul).

Hargreaves, J. (ed.) (1985) 'Their Own Worst Enemies', *Sport and Leisure*, July–August, pp. 20–8.

Harper, J. and Richards, L. (1979) *Mothers and Working Mothers* (Harmondsworth: Penguin).

Harrison, B. (1971) *Drink and the Victorians: The Temperance Question in England 1815–1872* (London: Faber).

Hearn, J. (1987) *The Gender of Oppression – Men, Masculinity and the Critique of Marxism* (Brighton: Wheatsheaf).

Heron, L. (1986) *Changes of Heart: Reflection on Women's Independence* (London: Pandora).

Hey, V. (1986) *Patriarchy and Pub Culture* (London: Tavistock).

Herzberg, F. (1986) *Work and the Nature of Man* (New York: Crowell).

Hobsbawm, E. (1960) *Industry and Empire* (Harmondsworth: Penguin).

Hobson, D. (1978) 'Housewives: Isolation as Oppression', in Women's Studies Group, Centre for Contemporary Cultural Studies, *Women Take Issue: Aspects of Women's Subordination* (London: Hutchinson).

Hobson, D. (1981) 'Now That I'm Married . . .', in McRobbie, A. and McCabe, T., *Feminism for Girls* (London: Routledge and Kegan Paul).

Hoggart, R. (1958) *The Uses of Literacy* (Harmondsworth: Penguin).

Hooks, B. (1982) *'Ain't I a Woman?': Black Women and Feminism* (London: Pluto).

Hough, M. and Mayhew, P. (1985) *Taking Account of Crime: Key Findings from The 1984 British Crime Survey* (London: HMSO).

Huizinga, J. (1950) *Homo Ludens: A Study of the Play Element in Culture* (London: Routledge and Kegan Paul).

Hunt, P. (1980) *Gender and Class Consciousness* (London: Macmillan).

Hunt, G. and Saterlee, S. (1987) 'Darts, Drink and the Pub: The Culture of Female Drinking', *Sociological Review*, August.

Hutter, B. and Williams, G. (eds) (1981) *Controlling Women: The Normal and the Deviant* (London: Croom Helm).

Imray, L. and Middleton, A. (1983) 'Public and Private: Marking the Boundaries', in Gamarnikow, E. *et al.* (eds) *The Public and the Private* (London: Heinemann).

Institute of Leisure and Amenity Management (1986) *The ILAM Best Practice Series: The Leicester Experience*, ILAM.

Jayaratne, T. (1983) 'The Value of Quantitative Methodology for Feminist Research', in Bowles, G. and Duelli Klein, R. (eds) *Theories of Women's Studies* (London: Routledge and Kegan Paul).

Jerrome, D. (1984) 'Good Company: Elderly Women's Use of Time', paper presented at the Leisure Studies Association First International Conference on Leisure: Politics, Planning and People, University of Sussex.

Johnson, R. (1979) 'Histories of Culture/Theories of Ideology: Notes on an Impasse', in Barrett, M., Corrigan, P., Kuhn, A. and Wolff, J. (eds) *Ideology and Cultural Production* (London: Croom Helm).

Johnson, R. (1987) 'Leisure Studies as Cultural Studies: Critical Approaches', in Meijer, E. (ed.) *Everyday Life; Leisure and Culture*, Dutch Centre for Leisure Studies, Tilburg University, The Netherlands.

Kirkham, J. (1987) 'Hidden Assets: The Use of Domestic Resources in Small Businesses', Research note presented to the Tenth National Small Firms Policy and Research conference.

Land, H. (1983) 'Poverty and Gender: The Distribution of Resources within the Family', in Brown, M. (ed.) *The Structure of Disadvantage* (London: Heinemann).

Lees, S. (1986) *Losing Out: Sexuality and Adolescent Girls* (London: Hutchinson).

Lembright, M. and Riemer, J. (1982) 'Women Truckers' Problems and the Impact of Sponsorship', *Work and Occupations*, vol. 9, no. 4.

Lewis, J. (1984) *Women in England 1870–1950* (Brighton, Sussex: Wheatsheaf Books).

Liff, S. (1988) 'Gender, Office Work and Technological Change', paper presented at the PICT/WICT Workshop, March 1988, Bath University.

Litman, G. K. *et al.* (1976) 'Evaluation of the Female Alcoholic: A Study of Person Perception', in *Proceedings of Annual Conference of British Psychological Society*.

Llewelyn Davies, M. (ed.) (1978) *Maternity: Letters from Working Women* (London: Virago).

Lloyd, N. (1985) 'Motivations and Remedies: Examples of Good Practice', in *Women and Sport: Report on a Seminar* (Leeds: Sports Council, Yorkshire and Humberside Regional Office).

London Borough of Hackney (1987) *Women in Leisure* (London: Community Services Unit, Department of Leisure Services, Shoreditch Town Hall).

Lorber, J. (1984) *Women Physicians – Careers, Status and Power* (London: Tavistock).

Lynd, R. and Lynd, H. M. (1929) *Middletown: A Study in American Culture* (New York: Harcourt Brace, Jovanovich).

McCabe, T. (1981) 'Girls and Leisure', in Tomlinson, A. (ed.) *Leisure and Social Control* (Brighton: Brighton Polytechnic).

McGregor, D. (1960) *The Human Side of the Enterprise* (New York: McGraw-Hill).

McIntosh, S. (1981) 'Leisure Studies and Women', in Tomlinson, A. (ed.) *Leisure and Social Control* (Brighton: Brighton Polytechnic).

McKee, L. and Bell, C. (1983) 'Marital and Family Relations in Times of Male Unemployment', in Finnegan, R. *et al.* (eds) *New Approaches to the Sociology of Economic Life* (Manchester: Manchester University Press).

McKee, L. and Bell, C. (1986) 'His Unemployment: Her Problem. The Domestic and Marital Consequences of Male Unemployment' in Allen, S. *et al.* (eds) *The Experience of Unemployment* (London: Macmillan).

McNally, F. (1979) *Women For Hire: A Study of the Female Office Worker* (London: Macmillan).

McRobbie, A. (1978) 'Working Class Girls and the Culture of Femininity', in Women's Studies Group, Centre for Contemporary Cultural Studies, *Women Take Issue* (London: Hutchinson).

McRobbie, A. (1982) 'Jackie: An Ideology of Adolescent Femininity' in Waites, N., Bennett, T. and Martin, G. (eds) *Popular Culture: Past and Present* (London: Croom Helm and Open University Press).

McRobbie, A. and Garber, J. (1976) 'Girls and Subcultures: An Exploration', in Hall, S. and Jefferson, T. (eds), *Resistance Through Rituals: Youth Subcultures in Post-war Britain* (London: Hutchinson).

MackSmith, A. and Stewart, D. G. (1984) *Women and Recreation: A Survey of Local Authority Policies and Provision* (Leicester: Planning and Research Section, Recreation and Arts Department, Leicester City Council).

Mason, J. (1988) 'No Peace for the Wicked: Older Married Women and Leisure', in Wimbush, E. and Talbot, M. (eds) *Relative Freedoms: Women and Leisure* (Milton Keynes: Open University Press).

Miller, B. (1986) 'Conflict and Violence among Alcoholic Women as Compared to a Random Sample of Women', paper presented to 38th Annual meeting of American Society of Criminology, Atlanta, Georgia, October.

Mitchell, J. and Oakley, A. (1986) *What is Feminism?* (Oxford: Blackwell).

Mitchell, S. (1975) 'The Policeman's Wife – Urban and Rural', *The Police Journal*, vol. 48, pp. 79–88.

Morris, L. (1984) 'Redundancy and Household Finance', *Sociological Review*, August.

Morris, L. (1985) 'Local Social Networks and Domestic Organisation', *Sociological Review*, May.

Mumford, E. and Sademan, H. (1975) *Human Choice and Computers 2*, conference proceedings, edited by Abbe Mowfchowitz (Oxford: North Holland Publishing Co.).

Myrdal, J. and Klein, V. (1956) *Women's Two Roles: Home and Work* (London: Routledge and Kegan Paul).

Nava, M. (1984) 'Youth Service Provision, Social Order and the Question of Girls', in McRobbie, A. and Nava, M. (eds) *Gender and Generation* (London: Macmillan).

Newton, J. and Rosenfelt, D. (1985) *Feminist Criticism and Social Change* (London: Methuen).

NOP Market Research Ltd (1983) 'Leisure Activities', in *Political, Social, Economic Review*, no. 43, September, pp. 12–20.

Oakley, A. (1974) *The Sociology of Housework* (Oxford: Martin Robertson).

Oakley, A. (1984) *Taking It Like A Woman* (London: Cape).

Otto, S. (1981) 'Women, Alcohol and Social Control', in Hutter, B. and Williams, G. (eds) *Controlling Women: The Normal and the Deviant* (London: Croom Helm).

Pahl, J. and Pahl, R. (1971) *Managers and Their Wives: A Study of Career and Family Relationships in the Middle Class* (Harmondsworth: Penguin).

Pahl, J. (1984) 'The Allocation of Money within the Household', in Freeman, M. (ed.) *The State, the Law and the Family* (London: Tavistock).

Parker, S. (1971) *The Future of Work and Leisure* (London: Paladin).

Parker, S. (1976) *The Sociology of Leisure* (London: Allen and Unwin).

Parker, S. (1983) *Leisure and Work* (London: Allen and Unwin).

Parker, S. (1985) *Leisure and the Elderly in London*, papers in Leisure Studies, No. 11 (London: Polytechnic of North London).

Parker, S., Brown, R. K., Child, P. and Smith, M. A. (1972) *The Sociology of Industry* (London: Allen and Unwin).

Parkin, F. (1971) *Class, Inequality and Political Order* (London: McGibbon and Kee).

Patterson, S. (1965) *Dark Strangers: A Study of West Indians in London* (Harmondsworth: Penguin).

Pearson, V. (1986) 'Management Report: Charteris Community Sports Centre, December 1985 – March 1986', Unpublished report.

Perkins, T. (1979) 'Re-Thinking Stereotypes', in Barrett, M. *et al.* (eds) *Ideology and Cultural Production* (New York: St. Martins).

Pollert, A. (1981) *Girls, Wives, Factory Lives* (London: Macmillan).

Pollock, G. (1977) 'What's Wrong with Images of Women', *Screen Education*, no. 24.

Purcell, K. (1979) 'Militancy and Acquiescence among Women Workers' in Burman, S. (ed.) *Fit Work for Women* (London: Croom Helm).

Radford, J. (1985) 'Policing Male Violence – Policing Women', paper presented to the BSA Annual Conference, University of Hull.

Ramazanoglu, C. (1986) 'Ethnocentrism and Socialist–Feminist Theory: A Response to Barrett and McIntosh', *Feminist Review*, no. 22.

Ramazanoglu, C. (1989) *Feminism and the Contradictions of Oppression* (London: Routledge and Kegan Paul).

Rapoport, R. and Rapoport, R. (1975) *Leisure and the Family Life Cycle* (London: Routledge and Kegan Paul).

Rapoport, R. and Rapoport, R. (1976) *Dual-Career Families Re-examined* (Oxford: Martin Robertson).

Rapoport, R., Fogarty, M. and Rapoport, R. (eds) (1982) *Families in Britain* (London: Routledge and Kegan Paul).

Reid, D. A. (1986) The Decline of Saint Monday 1766–1876', in Thane, P. and Sutcliffe, A., *Essays in Social History, vol.*II, Oxford: Clarendon Press.

Rigg, M. (1986) *Action Sport. Community Sports Leadership in the Inner Cities: An Evaluation* (London: Sports Council).

Roberts, E. (1984) *A Woman's Place* (Oxford: Blackwell).

Roberts, H. (1981) *Doing Feminist Research* (London: Routledge and Kegan Paul).

Roberts, K. (1970) *Leisure* (London: Longman).

Roberts, K. (1978) *Contemporary Society and the Growth of Leisure* (London: Longman).

Roberts, K. (1983) *Youth and Leisure* (London: Allen and Unwin).

Rogers, B. (1984) 'Men Only, Please', *New Statesman*, 3 February.

Rojek, C. (1985) *Capitalism and Leisure Theory* (London: Tavistock).

Rowbotham, S. (1973) *Hidden From History* (London: Pluto Press).

Rowbotham, S. (1979) 'The Trouble with Patriarchy', *New Statesman*, 98.

Saifullah Khan, V. (ed.) (1979) *Minority Families in Britain: Support and Stress. Studies in Ethnicity* (London: Macmillan).

Salaman, G. (1974) *Community and Occupation* (Cambridge: Cambridge University Press).

Sandmaier, M. (1980) *The Invisible Alcoholics: Women and Alcohol Abuse in America* (New York: McGraw Hill).

Saunders, B. (1980) 'Psychological Aspects of Women and Alcohol', (Camberwell Council on Alcoholism).

Scase, R. and Goffee, R. (1982) 'Homelife in a Small Business', in Evans, M. (ed.) *The Woman Question: Readings on the Subordination of Women* (London: Fontana).

Science Policy Research Unit (1982) *Women and Technology Studies: Microelectronics and Women's Employment in Britain*, Occasional Papers Series, No. 17, SPRU, University of Sussex (Brighton: Falmer).

Scraton, S. (1986) 'Images of Femininity and the Teaching of Girls' Physical Education', in Evans, J. (ed.) *Physical Education, Sport and Schooling* (Brighton: Falmer Press).

Scraton, S. (1987) 'Boys Muscle in Where Angels Fear to Tread: The Relationship between Physical Education and Young Women's Subcultures', in Jary, D., Horne, J. and Tomlinson, A. (eds) *Sociological Review Monograph*, no. 33 (London: Routledge and Kegan Paul).

Seiter, E. (1986) 'Feminism and Ideology: The Terms of Women's Stereotypes', *Feminist Review*, no. 22, Spring.

Sharpe, S. (1976) *Just Like a Girl* (Harmondsworth: Penguin).

Sharpe, S. (1984) *Double Identity: The Lives of Working Mothers* (Harmondsworth: Penguin).

Shaw, S. (1986) 'Gender and Leisure: Inequality in the Distribution of Leisure Time', *Journal of Leisure Research, vol.*17, no. 4, pp. 266–82.

Slater, E. and Woodside, M. (1951) *Patterns of Marriage* (London: Cassell).

Smart, C. and Smart, B. (1978) *Women, Sexuality and Social Control* (London: Routledge and Kegan Paul).

Smith, R. (1976) 'Sex and Occupational Role on Fleet Street', in Barker, D. Leonard and Allen, S. (eds) *Dependence and Exploitation in Work and Marriage* (London: Longman).

Sofer, C. (1970) *Men in Mid-Career* (Cambridge: Cambridge University Press).

Spender, D. (1981) *Men's Studies Modified: The Impact of Feminism on the Academic Disciplines* (Oxford: Pergamon).

Sports Council (1982) *Sport in the Community: The Next Ten Years* (London: Sports Council).

Sports Council (1984) *Participation: Taking Up the Challenge* (London: Sports Council).

Sports Council (1986) *Women and Sport: Report on a Seminar* (Leeds: Sports Council, Yorkshire and Humberside Regional Office).

Spring Rice, M. (1939) *Working Class Wives* (Harmondsworth: Penguin).

SPRU (1982) *Women and Technology Studies: Microelectronics and Women's Employment in Britain*, Science Policy Research Unit, University of Sussex, Occasional Papers Series No. 17.

Stanko, E. (1985) *Intimate Intrusions* (London: Routledge and Kegan Paul).

Stanley, L. (1980) *The Problem of Women and Leisure: An Ideological Construct and a Radical Feminist Alternative*, paper produced for the Sports Council/SSRC Joint Panel on Sport and Leisure and Recreation Research (London: Sports Council).

Stockdale, J. (1985) *What is Leisure? An Empirical Analysis of the Concept of Leisure and the Role of Leisure in People's Lives* (London: Sports Council).

Talbot, M. (1979) *Women and Leisure*, paper produced for the Sports Council/SSRC Joint Panel on Sport and Leisure and Recreation Research (London: Sports Council).

Taylor, J. (1986) 'The Pram People: Toddlers and Parents in Leisure Provision', paper presented to the Annual Conference of the Institute of Baths and Recreation Managers.

Theberge, N. (1981) 'A Critique of Critiques: Radical and Feminist Writings on Sport', in *Social Forces*, vol. 60, no. 2, pp. 341–53.

Thompson, E. P. (1968) *The Making of the English Working Class* (Harmondsworth: Penguin).

Thompson, P. (1975) *The Edwardians* (London: Weidenfeld and Nicolson).

Thompson, J. (1983) *Learning Liberation* (London: Croom Helm).

Tomlinson, A. (ed.) *Leisure and Social Control* (Brighton: Brighton Polytechnic).

Veal, A. (1987) *Leisure and the Future*, Leisure and Recreation Studies 4 (London: Allen and Unwin).

Volst, A. and Wagner, I. (1986) 'Meaningful Use of Computers in the Office: Automation Practices and their Organizational Framework', paper presented at the European conference on Women, Natural Science and Technology. November 1986, Elsinore, Denmark.

Walby, S. (1983) 'Flexibility and the Sexual Division of Labour', paper presented to the Conference on Part-Time Work, WYCROW, University of Bradford.

Walker, L. E. (1986) 'The Battered Women Syndrome Study', in Finkelhor, D. *et al.*, *The Dark Side of Families: Current Family Violence Research* (Beverly Hills: Sage).

Walvin, J. (1978) *Leisure and Society 1830–1950* (London: Longman).

Warrington, J. and White, A. (1986) *Sport and Recreation for Women and Girls: An Action Guide for Providers* (London: Sports Council).

Wearing, B. and Wearing, S. (1988) '"All in a Day's Leisure": Gender and the Concept of Leisure', *Leisure Studies*, 7, pp. 111–123.

Weeks, J. (1986) *Sexuality* (London: Ellis Horwood and Tavistock).

Weir, M. (1977) 'Are Computer Systems and Humanised Work Compatible?' in Ottoway, R.N., *Humanising the Workplace* (London: Croom Helm).

West, J. (ed.) (1982) *Women, Work and the Labour Market* (London: Routledge and Kegan Paul).

Westwood, S. (1984) *All Day Every Day: Factory and Family in the Making of Women's Lives* (London: Pluto).

White, C. (1970) *Women's Magazines 1693–1968* (London: Michael Joseph).

White, A. (1987) 'Take Me to Your Leader', *Sport and Leisure*, July–August, pp. 36–8.

Whitehead, A. (1976) 'Sexual Antagonism in Herefordshire', in Barker, D. L. and Allen, S. (eds) *Dependence and Exploitation in Work and Marriage* (London: Longman).

Williams, R. (1962) *Culture and Society* (Harmondsworth: Penguin).

Wilson, A. (1978) *Finding a Voice: Asian Women in Britain* (London: Virago).

Wilson, E. (1983) *What Is To Be Done About Violence Against Women* (Harmondsworth: Penguin).

Wimbush, E. (1986) *Women, Leisure and Well-Being: Final Report* (Edinburgh: Centre for Leisure Research, Dunfermline College of Physical Education).

Wimbush, E. and Talbot, M. (1988) *Relative Freedoms: Women and Leisure* (Milton Keynes: Open University Press).

Winship, J. (1978) 'A Woman's World: *Woman* - an Ideology of Femininity', in Women's Studies Group, Centre for Contemporary Cultural Studies *Women Take Issue: Aspects of Women's Subordination* (London: Hutchinson).

Winship, J. (1981) 'Handling Sex', in *Media, Culture and Society*, no. 3, pp. 25–41.

Winship, J. (1983) 'Femininity and Women's Magazines', in Unit 6, U221 *The Changing Experience of Women* (Milton Keynes: The Open University).

Wise, S. and Stanley, L. (1987) *Georgie Porgie: Sexual Harassment in Everyday Life* (London: Pandora).

Wood, J. (1984) 'Groping Towards Sexism: Boys' Sex Talk', in McRobbie, A. and Nava, M. (eds) *Gender and Generation* (London: Macmillan).

Woodward, D., Green, E. and Hebron, S. (1988) 'Bouncing the Balls Around . . . or Keeping Them in the Air? The Sociology of Women's Leisure and Physical Recreation', paper presented to the Second International Conference of the Leisure Studies Association, University of Sussex, Brighton.

Woodward, D., Green, E. and Hebron, S. (1989) 'The Sociology of Women's Leisure and Physical Recreation', paper presented at the International Congress on Movement and Sport in Women's Life, University of Jyväskylä, Finland, and subsequently published in the *International Review for the Sociology of Sport*.

Young, M. and Willmott, P. (1957) *Family and Kinship in East London* (London: Routledge and Kegan Paul).

Young, M. and Willmott, P. (1973) *The Symmetrical Family: Study of Work and Leisure in the London Region* (London: Routledge and Kegan Paul).

Index